UPGRADE YOURSELF

Thru The Holistic Movement

• •

Your Life Guide To Self- Mastery

By:

JULIE RAMMAL

"Your body is an empire, when you are connected to you, you can achieve miracles."
–Julie Rammal

"Life Is Amazing, Only Re-Affirm It."
–Julie Rammal

AuthorHouse™
1663 Liberty Drive
Bloomington, IN 47403
www.authorhouse.com
Phone: 833-262-8899

This book is printed on acid-free paper.

ISBN: 978-1-6655-3055-2 (sc)
978-1-6655-3056-9 (e)

Library of Congress Control Number: 2021913237

Print information available on the last page.

Published by AuthorHouse 12/15/2021

authorHOUSE®

UPGRADE YOURSELF

Thru The Holistic Movement

INTRODUCTION

"The kingdom of heaven is within you, and whomsoever shall know himself shall find it."
-Egyptian proverb

This book grants you the key to re-connect, empower and ignite, through the Holistic Movement, the amazing power of body, mind, and soul.

The Holistic Movement shares the power of re-connecting our body, mind and soul to a higher source of Divine power, and to live and move our bodies in connection and harmony with nature and the universe. The Holistic methodology offers practices and exercises to re-enlighten humanity by teaching how to acquire and maintain a balanced, empowered, positive, and harmonious inner system that is fully aligned with the outer energy sources and supremacies of the universe.

The methodology honours and builds on the ancestors' cumulative knowledge to date. It respects the laws of nature and the universe. It offers: education, discipline, mastery, and training for the body, mind and soul, to re-strengthen and synchronize them to the outer energy of the universe. It shares the strength of our being, creation, purpose, love, self-healing and gives individuals the knowledge and power to safely and smoothly transform in the new undefined era. The Holistic methodology prepares humans to cope with upcoming changes and surmount future challenges.

The power of the Holistic methodology is founded on love, and opens the door to all to have joy, love, happiness, healing, and youthful energy and positivity. The utmost benefits will become clear to those who follow the Holistic methodology concepts, acquire knowledge, and put them into practice.

There are many different answers as to who is a human being or who we all are. The nature of the human specie is extraordinary and astonishing. Defining it significantly varies in texts and dictionaries. For example, the definition of a human being according to <u>Encyclopaedia Britannica</u>, is "Human being, a culture-bearing primate classified in the genus *Homo*, especially the species *H. sapiens*. Human beings are anatomically similar and related to the great apes but are distinguished by a more highly developed brain and a resultant capacity for articulate speech and abstract reasoning. In addition, human beings display a marked erectness of body carriage that frees the hands for use as manipulative members." On the other hand, the Holistic methodology and Taoism share another different and common definition of what the human specie is. In both philosophies, the human specie is believed to create and find their path to be in union with the universe.

The Holistic methodology teaches people to maintain an inner-harmony between the body, mind, and soul and to build a strong connection and alignment with the universe. As such, humans should not engage in activities that disrupt this connection that will be harmful for us, as individuals, and could be destructive to wider communities and the entire world. Consequently, humans should engage in activities that make the world a more energetic, positive, and healthier place to live in.

We can all live an amazing life filled with self-unity, joy, love, health, youthfulness, energy, and connection to ourselves and the world, if we could bring awareness on how to ignite the wonderous powers available to us, and revive our connection to ourselves, nature, and to the outer universe.

The world will open its arms to humans who know who they are and to those who are connected within in body, mind, soul, and to the outer-universe. Those individuals honor humanity, understand and apply the laws of nature, and conform to the universal code of harmony and conduct. Consequently, all humans could easily live a harmonious life full of energy and joy.

"Re-connection, self-mastery, and owning our body, mind and soul will give one immense abundance, joy, health, and love to surpass all challenges."

-Julie Rammal

According to numerous researches, the human specie may soon devolve, evolve slightly, or completely transform into a new specie. One key contributor to these major shifts, is the rapid rise of technology and human's increased dependency on it, making it soon be intertwined within us unknowingly. Ben Goertzel, American author and researcher predicts that in 2045, we are going to merge with technology whether we want it or not.

For thousands of years, the human specie lived and was connected to nature. Everything was built by connection, observation, and studying the world and the universe. The supremacy of our re-connection to nature, animals, the universe, and ourselves should be enhanced to remember that we are all connected and in union with everything inside and outside of ourselves. Today, for example, the only common traits that we share with our ancestors is a slightly evolved body and super evolved conscious mind. Our present body, mind, and movements have taken a 320 degree turn within the past 200 years as technology gave birth. The technological revolution, has altered humans to mostly use their conscious minds, rather than our subconscious minds. The conscious mind is the weakest organ that only constitutes 5% of our brain, while our subconscious mind has around 95% of the power. Our use of conscious mind has affected the majority of the world's population and spread: anxiety, depression, stress, lack of vision or purpose, and suffering in body and mind. If we compare our minds and bodies to those who lived in the 80's, there is a remarkable difference in appearance, body, expression, and vibration. Today, we should reawaken ourselves, learn from history, and re-connect to the power of being positive, loving, kind, compassionate, and forgiving. These tools can change us and change our world, our perspective, the quality of our life, and our ultimate destination.

We should honour our ancestral knowledge, respect the laws of nature and the universe, and re-connect in body, mind, and soul. Resistance of this natural flow will only create greed, ego, selfishness, negative emotions, actions, illnesses and so forth. The Holistic methodology allows one to re-connect to a higher source of power, and to live a balanced and harmonious inner and outer life.

Many of our external systems are vacuuming us away from ourselves, and then throwing gadgets for us to adapt to when everything around us is changing faster than the human specie can adapt to. Currently, and in the past 30 years, we are now inter-connected to nearly 1-6 electronic devices such as: computers, ipads, cell phones, drones, ear plugs and other gadgets. The majority of people are allowing these devices to consume their: body, mind and soul, and are even replacing real human friends with virtual friends. Our dependency on technology will increase and be intertwined within our entire system, if we do not learn how to use and re-evaluate technology. Most of us have felt the negative mental and physical effects of technology such as: mood swings, anxiety, lack of focus, altered emotions and behaviour, depression, loneliness, stress, and so forth. It can be an addiction. If one does not know how to use technology for one's benefit, one could become unwillingly drugged into some technological applications and gadgets. Today, we can sense the effects, however; with more exposure, we may well soon lose this sense of feeling.

We need to increase our connection to nature, the emotion and feeling of love, self-mastery, and a deeper understanding of how to use technology only for our benefit, and not in a harmful ways. We must build our inner connection, learn how to keep our body, mind and soul well balanced, in order to remain positive, happy, and loving in this beautiful world.

In conclusion, allow us to listen and understand our world and follow its rules in order to enhance all life today and in the future. Our future depends on returning back to ourselves, ancestral knowledge, self- mastery, and using the Holistic methodology to guide us in the present and future. We must ignite our powers to surpass the future rise of diseases and viruses, poor immune system, and environmental challenges.

The Holistic methodology offers the training, education and discipline for our: body, mind, and soul to evolve in harmony with ourselves and everything around us. The Holistic methodology is to be used as your resource and guide to master and understand ourselves in the realms of super changes and evolution in the human specie.

The knowledge and philosophies in this book are precious, and should be used with guidance, gratitude and reverence. The acquired knowledge will enrich your life on all levels. Take from this book what resonates with you to enlighten and empower yourself and others and enrich what could be an amazing life journey.

"Eyes upward, feet forward, and hearts homeward."

-Five Legends (Native Americans)

Chapter 1:

The Power Of Change

If you have selected this book, be happy and smile because your calling or subconscious is guiding you to awaken, change, or transform something in your: body, mind, and life.

The Holistic methodology is the mastery of oneself to adapt to the upcoming changes that impact our: body, mind, and soul. The Holistic Movement offers internal and external: **awareness, education, training, discipline, and movement that combines an understanding of nature and the universe, ancient and modern science, body, mind, soul, and healing modalities to initiate the right changes to adapt to the new era.** This book is your survival guide to adapt into being a connected, enlightened, and aligned as the "future conscious human specie."

It is a book that revives the human specie with love and honors everything within our internal self.

To initiate the power of the Holistic methodology, one must make a decision to change and believe in that change. Everything in our world is constantly changing. In our present and future, change will become obligatory to survive. We can and deserve to be extremely happy, positive, and loving regardless of stress and our fast pace environment. The key is in using and mastering the Holistic methodology to honor, observe, listen, practice and re-connect oneself in body, mind, and soul to the universe.

Many of us have already experienced familiar or basic changes in life such as changes in: career, money, family, friends, location, social status, sports and diet, health, healing etc... However, in the near future we will be forced to adapt to changes that are beyond: emotional, cultural, economic, and social. We will be facing genetic modification of the human specie, less earth resources, higher prices, less jobs, increased stress, health and mental problems, broken family and social bonds, climate changes, uncurable diseases, natural disasters, global pandemics, shortage of clean water and nutritious food and more. Moreover; we may lose connection to being human and re-awakening our human powers. This change has already begun, as many of us can no longer access their: heart, emotions, feelings as technology seems to have grown inside the human body, mind and soul. The majority of new humans are controlled via technology, and it has become a luxury to be able to think, feel, move freely, and access one's emotions. It has become a rare emotion to be happy, loving, and alive in body, mind and soul. Alongside, many people are losing vision, purpose, and simply engaging in a robotic routine behaviour unconsciously. The Holistic Movement makes life re-appear: beautiful, joyful, loving, creative, healthy through the power of re-connecting body, mind and soul to the cosmos.

The world is rapidly changing, and we should re-awaken our powers to adapt to the new era. If we are not in control of ourselves and technology, our technology could become our own enemy. To surpass the future changes, it is important to master our inner worlds, honor ancestral knowledge, and to embrace and prepare oneself for the upcoming era.

Imagine in 2060, your new-born child is now genetically modified and born into a lab. The feeling of having a child would not be like the feeling a mother may have today. There may be no feelings between the human specie. The new-born's subconscious and brain are pre-programmed during a mother's pregnancy and at birth. The child is the state's or one government child that is programmed to follow certain robotic tasks. A chip is implanted in their brain and body, they are tattooed with an identification number, and some of their senses such as: sight, hearing, feeling, taste are removed at birth. Their entire mental, emotional and physical states are altered to follow the one state or government. If any signs of alternation are shown they are sent to a detention camp for re-programming or defect. Parents are kept away from their children, and children grow up as a robotic being programmed to follow the one government's duty and mission. Pills and medicine will no longer be the cure, the cure will be in high dose injections, implanted chips, chemically induced drugs, and genetic modification of the being. Skills such as: thinking, creativity, entrepreneurship, motivation, logic, sport, health, spirituality, and cognitive skills may soon vanish. **In the new upcoming era you must enhance and ignite your human powers.**

"The Holistic Movement re-awakens the human specie on all levels."
-Julie Rammal

Now, close your eyes, and feel your entire identity, freedom, health, body, mind and soul being altered to a controlled state as a new robotic specie. As you try to fight, and find yourself, every passion, dream, thought, belief, emotion is taken away from you. Imagine how would you feel if this change was forced upon you? What would it feel like to have no life?

Now, close your eyes, and feel your entire mind, body, and soul free, happy, energized, youthful, and connected to the universe, nature, and everything in the world.

The Holistic Movement is a movement that opens the doors to having a beautiful, joyous, and connected life in body, mind, and soul with oneself, nature, and the universe. It gives one knowledge, and direction to fine tune one's self and life to adapt in present and to the future.

During the transition, many people may experience changes in body, mind, emotions, soul, and self. Such changes are already explicit today as: depression, mental issues, unhappiness, loneliness, eating disorders, and so forth. The Holistic methodology is one's home that offers happiness, love, positivity and connection to oneself to thrive and be empowered on all levels.

Be happy, you have selected a book that will be your genuine friend and guidance for life. You are that strong selected survivor, and the knowledge and skills that you acquire in this Book will enable you to enlighten other people's lives, a generation, and the future of the human specie. Pass the inherited knowledge to empower and awaken every generation with the light of change, love, joy, health, and connection to ourselves and the universe. Allow this light of power to spread benefit to the human race and world to join and follow an enhanced path of life.

This book was designed to teach each one of us our inner and external world, our inner power, gifts, and to shower us with awareness on how to train our: body, mind, emotions, and subconscious within the divine laws and fields of being human. The Holistic methodology gives you resources to create a: strong, disciplined, aware, and balanced self that is confident, empowered, happy, energized, and youthful.

Before we can undergo the Holistic methodology, we must understand the power of change. Most of us desire change yet fear it, because we are naturally habitual beings, and our minds and body love routine. The Holistic methodology empowers us to discover the unknown and build resilience against fear. It shows us the way to live a life internally fulfilled with: joy, natural confidence, curiosity, love, happiness, ambitions and to see everything as positive and amazing. All of this can be achieved with a re-trained mindset, discipline, repetition, and a natural body to house our mind and soul. Once one is internally well built, the external changes will have little impact on each individual. The richness of ourselves lies in ethics, values, kindness, compassion, love, honesty, and to be true within ourselves. The Holistic methodology will give you power of vision, mental clarity, emotional balance, physical flexibility, natural strength, and an inner communication system to work with yourself. The power of change lies within one thought, added value, belief, or action that will cause change to automatically follow.

"Your body is an empire, and when you are connected to yourself, you can achieve miracles."

-Julie Rammal

We cannot stop major external changes in our conscious world, as change is natural and a constant in life. Our universe and world are much bigger and stronger than us. We can only embrace change, and change within ourselves to manifest our external lives. We are a mirror of the universe, and everything that is within our body, mind, and soul is projected in our world. Imagine if you are swimming in the middle of the ocean with waves that are 3 meters high. You have 3 options: float for a certain period of time, panic and sink, or swim to survive. The Holistic methodology is your swimming lesson to embrace life, adapt to challenges and changes, and to survive. The power of knowing ourselves, gives us a power to re-create ourselves, and change our world. Change is a gift that should be welcomed, and should be seen as a tool to train deeper within ourselves to survive change. If the conditions of change are faster than our ability to evolve and adapt, the human specie will face major obstacles. If the mind, subconscious, heart, emotions, thoughts, beliefs, faith, self-awareness and self-communication, and body are not prepared for change, one will heavily struggle with the future changes that we will be faced with and be vacuumed into the force set of changes.

"It is the not the strongest or the most intelligent who will survive but those who can best manage change."

-Charles Darwin

Allow us to begin by purchasing a couple tickets before we get started. Your first ticket is your belief in your power to change. The second ticket, is your ticket to re-open your subconscious mind and minimize conscious mind usage. The third ticket is to engage, learn, and practice the Holistic philosophies, methodologies towards self mastery.

Allow us to begin to feel, have purpose, vision, emotions, mental clarity, physical health, and happiness today and onwards. You do not need to feel locked in the mass evolution of: suffering, loss of purpose, identity, feeling, mental, physical, emotional dis-balance, distress, confusion, soul rupture, and oppression anymore. You can begin living life with the subconscious mind, which constitutes 95% of our powers, versus the conscious mind, the weakest organ with only constitutes of only 5% of our brain powers. Our heart and subconscious are the strongest fields of power. We can live happy, stress free, healthy, and have an amazing balanced body, mind and soul again.

Every human being has the right to live a healthy, dis-ease free life filled with positivity, joy, and a feeling of being and belonging. Allow us to re-attach to our human powers, and being human. The Holistic methodology will help you choose and grow your own beliefs, and to form new habits for a positive transformed life. The Holistic methodology is your friend, and it is a movement to wake up the human population through: self study, awareness, communication, discipline, education, training, and re-aligning one's body, mind and soul with the universe and self. Your future is in your hands, and the Holistic methodology welcomes you to your new journey of self-mastery, control, discipline to live a positive, happy, and balanced life.

Birth Of A New Being

As the world is changing and evolving, humanity and the universe is giving birth to a more evolved version of itself that is being awakened. There are two directions that the human specie will be forced to take, road A or road B. Road A will lead to the evolution of the human being to be a controlled robotic specie. This specie will be highly connected to technology and semi or fully controlled in body, mind, and soul. They will not have any knowledge of themselves nor the outside world, as they are programmed to only perform tasks, jobs, duties. Road B will be the evolution of the human specie that regains ancestral knowledge, tools, awareness, and connection to their body, mind, soul, and the universe. This specie will practice natural forms of movement, training, Holistic methodology, and will be happy, energized, and youthful while they fulfil their life's missions. They will continue the human specie's heritage, and have a strong inner access to their internal systems, power, and healing. They will be awakened and connected in: body, mind, and soul to the universe. Children will again enjoy hearing the beautiful bed time stories and folktales, and parents and people will be kinder, open, loving, compassionate, and happy. It is important for one to decide which route they want to enter, make a decision, and begin to take a direction of action. Those who want to continue evolving to a new human specie must scrutinize past historical patterns in order to know where the human specie is heading to. They must know themselves in order to prepare for the new field that will be forced upon them. The first steps to engage in change is to truly believe that you have the power to change, and believe in the change that you are standing for. This belief must be deep within one's existence, breath, mind, and identity.

The Holistic methodology will give you all the tools to fly above all challenges, and to grow as a new-born child in a new amazing world. Own you own your will power to change, and start your journey with your second and third tickets, you will evolve with major abundance, happiness, joy, love, health, and life. The human population should evolve to "Become what is needed" as Ghandi once said. Now, is your chance to re-align, re-tune, and connect to your remarkable internal and external sources of the incredible power that you have.

"The code of evolution is inside of us."
-Julie Rammal

In summary, the power of change will begin once you make a decision that you want to change and believe that you can. Once this decision is made, this book will be your best friend for life, and generations to come.

"The secret of change is to focus all your energy on not fighting the old but building the new."
-Socrates

The Holistic methodology is the future of co-existing in the transitions that we will be forced to alter to. To begin your journey of change, all you need is to change one thing, a thought, or belief, an action, a value, a new affirmation, and then the entire change will ripple itself. These minor changes are as powerful as an airplane changing its route by 1 degree. With 1 degree, an airplane can end up in an entire different destination. Believe in your power to change, and your route will naturally change its destination. Your changes can be simple and small. For example, you can begin by changing: your waking hours, training outdoors, smiling more, or simply by beginning to act like the change you want to see.

Therefore, sign a contract between yourself stating:

I (your name)………..………………….have the power to awaken my subconscious mind and self. I have the power to change and control my body and mind and all within myself. I am that source of power. I trust and believe in myself, and the Holistic methodology to guide me through my inner and external journey in life.

Date:……………

Sign:……………

Chapter 2:

Holistic Principles & Philosophies

Now, that you have made the decision to change, it is important to learn and acquire understanding of important concepts integrated in the Holistic Methodology: Life Maze, Yin Yang, 5 Chinese Elements Philosophy, Macrocosm/ Microcosm, Ayurveda, Vesica Pisces, and Self-Discipline. These concepts are integrated in the Holistic Methodology and must be comprehended in order to fully engage in the practice.

These concepts and philosophies are vital to our learning and understanding about the universe, how the world works, ourselves, and how to live a balanced, connected, and harmonious life within and outside of ourselves.

Life Maze

The Holistic methodology has created the Life Maze concept that states: our life is in a maze. It consists of a series of passages that may confuse us into false turns, obstacles, and deceptions. Changes may erupt suddenly, and shocking or surprising challenges may arise. It is important to think out-of-the-box and connect with the idea of the Life Maze Concept. When we: know ourselves and destination, we are less likely to get absorbed and affected by external events that could put us out of balance and significantly impact our life. Our vision must be alive and projected in our minds every moment.

In our lifetime, one is thrown into, what I refer to, as the Life Maze which is full of many: challenges, dead ends, illusions, u-turns, deviations, and tests that may de-balance our: mental, physical, emotional, energetic and spiritual space. Consequently, one has to understand and practice how to maintain and regain harmony within oneself and the universe. Otherwise, one could be quickly vacuumed into side beliefs, thoughts, false illusions, and engage in wrong actions that are harmful or deflecting us from our vision. If one takes a wrong turn inside the Life Maze, one could get easily affected, and experience: depression, take substances, attract unhealthy experiences, become confused or disoriented, and experience emotional unbalanced actions. In the Holistic Methodology we train our inner core of body, mind, and soul to be balanced, protected, and aligned within and with our outer world, by mainly removing the outer shells formed over our: subconscious, body, mind, and soul.

In the Life Maze concept we live a stimulated game that has rules that are mainly taught and acquired from ancestral knowledge and experience. If we do not follow the rules, evolve, learn, and re-connect within and outside ourselves, we may hit the wall and get stuck. The more we understand this illusive life, that we live in, the more we could excel in the game by staying focused to win our battles until the end. We win and excel in our maze when we understand ourselves, the rules, and how to use our secret tools to progress.

Our tools are in our system and include: energy, vibration, thoughts, beliefs, subconscious, heart, emotions, feelings, our talents, body, mind, and soul. We must view ourselves without ego and have a child's mind with ancestral wisdom. The Life Maze concept teaches us to view ourselves as systems, living and interacting inside wider systems, where each system has its own life maze.

When we view ourselves as a sub-system of a wider system, we can begin: training, disciplining, and enriching our internal systems. Our systems work together to perform a task, and can be divided briefly as follows:

Organ Systems: Integumentary, muscular, skeletal, nervous, circulatory, lymphatic, respiratory, endocrine, urinary/excretory, reproductive and digestive.

Body Systems: Circulatory, Digestive, Excretory, Immune, Integumentary, Reproductive, Muscular, Nervous, Urinary, Skeletal.

Mind Systems: Conscious, Unconscious, Subconscious.

Once one understands the basics of their systems, they are trained to build an awareness leading to an inter-connection offered in a different classroom for each system. Let us examine our control system, the brain, because it is one of the most important systems that we can rapidly change. Based on Sigmund Freud, our mind is divided as shown in The Mental Iceberg Image below.

**Freud's Iceberg Theory of Human Mind, The Mental Iceberg,
By: Sigmund Freud, founder of Psychoanalysis**

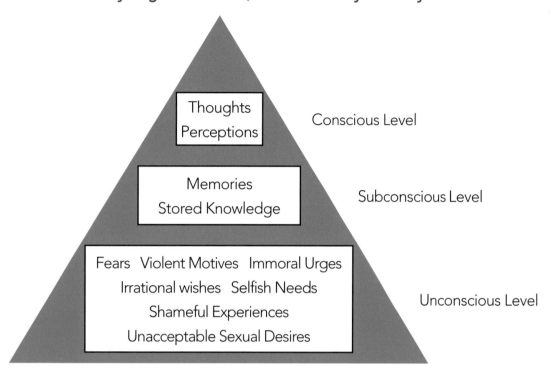

In the Holistic methodology, we view each part of the brain as a classroom. Therefore, we have three classrooms: the subconscious, conscious, and unconscious. As we age, these classrooms get filled up with many old files that may need reprogramming and fine tuning every so often.

Envision seeing these three classrooms. Within each classroom there are many students, all must be: awaken, re-trained, disciplined to become a new positive, balanced, and empowered student.

Our subconscious classroom is the largest and most important classroom, because it can change our reality if rewired. It is our main database or warehouse. *To change, we must clear our unconscious, and re-awaken our subconscious mind, to be aware of our conscious minds.*

- Within the **subconscious classroom** we have students that include:

    Beliefs, values, long term memories, habits, imagination, past thoughts, neglected subliminal information.

    Our subconscious classroom retrieves data from our unconscious classroom.

- Within the **unconscious classroom** we have the reservoir students that include:

    Repressed: feelings, fears, thoughts, instincts, superego, selfish motives, and past memories.

    Our conscious classroom retrieves *data and connects to the subconscious* classroom.

- Within the **conscious classroom** we have present moment students that include:

  Thoughts, short term memory, logical and critical thinking, wishes, awareness, perceptions.

In the Holistic methodology, building and understanding the classroom student concept helps us: re-program, re-train, re-discipline and comprehend how our mind and body work. With such communication skills, you can begin to direct yourself and systems frequently on: lifting their energy and vibration, instructing them what you want, where you are going, your vision, and develop a strategy how to get there in this Life Maze.

If you do not know how to get there, simply begin by weighing in the value of events, people, and things that come into your life. Constantly ask yourself, "Does this add value to my vision or life? Can I take it with me? Is this good for me? Do I need this thought? Do I need this emotion? Does this belief support my vision? Do I need it to get there?" You must constantly scan your inner inventory, be a brave warrior, trust your instinctive hearts' feelings, and grow your: body, mind and soul. In Chapter 4, we will discover the subconscious mind further.

Moreover, the rules to survive the Life Maze are:

1. Know yourself in and out
2. Own, feel, see your vision
3. Map a plan how to get to your vision
4. Gather and Master your skills
5. Master your inner systems
6. Master your golden tools: energy, vibration, heart, subconscious, thought, belief, emotions, feeling, mind, body, soul, own talents, awareness, control, self-discipline, persistence
7. Gain knowledge and skills
8. Be wary of distractions and surroundings
9. Rely on yourself
10. Trust yourself
11. Abide by the code of the heart and universe
12. Look for signs, hidden messages, meanings that come your way
13. Be kind, loving, compassionate, forgiving, and open
14. Do good, and good will follow
15. Be grateful
16. Listen more and talk less
17. Be humble

We are all on Earth to share a certain talent and abide to the code of the universe and heart. Those who do not abide, may fall ill, or experience dis-balance in body, mind and soul. The more you are self-aware and connect deeper within yourself, the faster you can: see, live, and feel your vision, propel and grow. Visionary powers excel us in our journey onto our Life Maze. Think of vision as having super power glasses to clear and see our life journey.

Unfortunately, many of us are lost in our maze, stagnant, afraid, or turning in viscous circles with negative emotions, thoughts, and beliefs. It almost seems as if life has become so difficult to continue to be happy and a good person. However; this is not true. We are happiest when we are truly love, connected, and satisfied and connected within ourselves. The Holistic Methodology will allow your new empowered actions, beliefs, character, and thoughts to shine bright.

Therefore, be yourself, follow the rules, and eliminate fear. Engage in internal and external energy cleansing, and lift your vibration or frequency daily. If our energy and vibrations are high, we experience health, joy, mental clarity, energy, and positive emotions, thoughts, and behaviours. If our energy and vibrations go low, we may gain negative emotions, behaviours, thoughts, sickness, and go the wrong way in our maze or hit another dead end path.

As we will see in the next section, Yin and Yang, disturbed Yin and Yang balance can put us off track. We must have the Yang of bravery and positivity with the Yin of calmness to win our Life Maze. Practicing and following the rules of: self-control, self-discipline, vision, positive attitude, thought, skill, action, persistence, and inner and outer connection to us and our world are needed to excel on our paths in our journey towards our vision. Once you reach the end, you won your vision.

In summary, know yourself, follow the rules, know and construct your Life Maze and prepare for it.

Yin Yang

The Yin Yang concept and symbol is one of the most well-known and oldest Chinese principles that was taught. It roots back to Taoism/ Daoism. In Chinese cosmology, the universe is believed to have been created from chaos of solid energy that was systematized into Yin, the extensive resources of life, and Yang, the motivating force that works with Yin's resources.

The first philosophical reference of Yin Yang appeared during the Han Dynasty, which lasted from 3rd century B.C. until 3rd century AD, and was associated with Wuxing, the five elements. The Wuxing and its teaching was the Chineses' first attempt to explain metaphysics and cosmology. Ying Yang and Wuxing have created a new system of thought that has incredibly influenced Chinese medicine, scientific approaches, martial arts, tai chi, qi gong, and other systems for thousands of years.

Chinese Five Elements (Wood, Fire, Earth, Metal, Water)

The Wuxing or 5 elements are: metal, wood, water, fire and earth. They are also forces, energies, and stages in the universe that decipher how the 5 elements interact, transform, and move everything in the cosmos. This concept is further explained under the Chinese 5 Element Philosophy in the next section in this chapter.

In the following Dynasty, Zhou Dynasty the Yin Yang was illustrated in connection with Qi (vital energy) and it was conceptualized further with famous Chinese philosophers, such as Lao Tzu and Confucius. The Confucian philosophy used the Yin Yang concept to explain the universe, and believed that Yin and Yang created the Tao, the source of all human and divine. Within the Tao, Qi was created. Confucians favoured the Yang while Taoist's preferred the calm Yin. Qi was perceived through Yin and Yang, and exist in the natural and human worlds.

Yin and Yang references appeared between 7-11th centuries B.C in the Shijing Chinese book of poetry, and the I Ching or Book of Changes, written by King Wen in the 9th century BCE during the Western Zhou dynasty. Additional Yin and Yang references have been discovered on engravings on oracle bones and animal skeletal remains. The engravings exhibited Day as Yang, and night as Yin in the 14th century B.C.E.

The concept of Yin and Yang was extremely popular in 3rd century BCE in the Chinese School Of Yin Yang. The Yin Yang concept express dualism, and harmonizing forces that interact to form a dynamic system in the greater scope of the world.

Yin Yang Symbol

The black and white colours in the Yin and Yang are opposites yet complimentary, and create a constant shared attraction and repulsion that causes constant change that is manifested in the universe.

Yin, is the matter, the dark tinted shadow referred to as negative, while Yang, is the action force, that is the bright white shadow referred to as positive. The Yin Yang symbol is composed of two large opposite color swirls, and have smaller dots of the opposite color inside of each swirl.

The inner small dots represent that everything contains the seed of the opposite. Yin and Yang are: oppositional forces, interdependent, can creatively transform each other, and can equally consume the other as it becomes predominant.

Yin = Dark, Negative, Empty, Low, Cold

Yang = Light, Growth, Positive, Warmth, Fullness, Aggressiveness, Speed

Yin and Yang are manifested everywhere on Earth, such as in the cycles of life, life/death, seasons, winter/ summer. Other examples: a waves crust is Yang and the trough is Yin; the sunbeam is Yang, while the shadows are Yin. An eggshell is Yang, and the egg inside is Yin. An introvert personality is Yin, while an extrovert personality is Yang.

Additional examples of Yin and Yang include: contract/expand, hard/soft, fire/water, chaos/ order, sleep/awake, dark/light, inner/outer, cold/ hot, low/high, flat/ round, matter/ energy, rest/ activity, interior/ exterior, front/ back, and so forth. In our pre-determined behaviours, we see the effect of Yin and Yang as well. For example, if we try very hard to be beautiful we become the opposite, an obsession over living can cause fear and obsession of dying. If we have a lot of possessions, we could become greedy, and if we have only a few we could become thieves. In addition, some personalities are introvert while others are extrovert. Both Yin and Yang create totality, and are needed to be whole. Yin and Yang can influence each other because both contain the opposite energy force inside of them. When two things are balanced, they are equal yet separate. Everything is always balancing and rebalancing into a state of harmony and follows the Yin and Yang philosophy.

In Taoism, nature has its own self balancing system, and it is believed that change will happen alone if required. We must understand this concept to execute balanced behaviours, emotions, thoughts, and actions. Taoism teaches us that we must learn from both Yin and Yang, and live in harmony with nature, rather than against nature's flow of life. For example, if we feel very healthy, we may not think of health and wellness at all. Our body, mind, emotions, and soul can be adjusted to our life circumstances. The Holistic methodology works on promoting this internal harmony to remain balanced through body and mind practices. For example, in the Holistic methodology, if someone is very stressed and the outside temperature is very hot, one may engage in a more Yin workout for their body and mind in order to avoid creating excess Yang. The Holistic methodology always focuses to harmonize body, mind and soul within oneself and the universe. As a result, every Holistic Movement session or consultation is never the same, and can be influenced by: time, day, energy, environment, weather, temperature, season, student's present state of body and mind and so forth.

The Four States of Yin and Yang Imbalance are:

1. Excess of Yin
2. Excess of Yang
3. Deficiency of Yin
4. Deficiency of Yang

Any excesses and deficiencies in Yin and Yang lead to disruption of Qi, the vital energy, which affects the state of one's body and mind. External disruptions or excesses in weather can also affect Qi. For example, if the weather changes abruptly from hot to cold, or sun to rain and so forth this can affect one's health and Qi. Other sources of disharmony include: trauma, over- exertion, excessive sexual activity, poor diet, poisons, parasites, or congenital weak constitutions at birth, or birth defects.

The Holistic methodology honors the Yin Yang concept to teach us how to remain harmonious and balanced within ourselves to restore and maintain health in body and mind. Connection to ourselves, nature, and the universe are vital for health and to live a harmonious holistic life. Nature possesses all of our answers and remedies, and has been the home for thousands of organisms, species, including ourselves for millions of years.

"Being and non- being produce each other.

Difficult and easy complement each other.

Long and short define each other.

High and low oppose each other.

Fore and aft follow each other."

-Lao Tzu, Tao Te Ching, Chapter 2 (Translated by John H. McDonald)

Yin Yang and The Human Body

The principles of Yin and Yang are fundamental to know and to have a balanced body and mind. The three major Yin and Yang systems for our health are: The Five Vital, Zang- Fu, and Jing- Lua.

The Five Vital are: Qi, Xue (Blood), Jinye (Body Fluids), Jing (Essence), and Shen (Spirit). There descriptions are as follows:

1. Qi, life energy, flows through the Jing-Lua (meridians). If Qi's pathways are disturbed disease or illness may prevail.
2. Xue, or blood, is the liquid life force of the body. Its' prime function is circulation. All Zang-Fu organs are nourished by Qi.
3. *Jinye, thick liquids that lubricate organs such as the brain. Distributed as nutrition to the body from consumption of liquids and foods.*
4. Jing, spirit of immaterial soul and physical body of person. Regulates body growth and development, works with Qi to protect the body from external factors. Jing and Qi are believed to form the Shen or spirit.
5. Shen, spirit is located in the heart, nourished by Xue. If unbalanced one can experience: mental illnesses, anxiety, extreme depression, or insomnia.

The second major Yin and Yan system for health is Zang-Fu.

Zang-Fu is a collection of 5 organs that control and create Qi in the body, and follow the Wuxing or 5 elements patterns. Zang are organs that are Yin in nature and consist of: pericardium, heart, liver, spleen, lung, kidneys. Fu are organs that are Yang in nature and consist of: triple burner, small intestine, large intestine, gall bladder, urinary bladder, stomach.

Xuxing and Zang- Fu Organs

Element	Wood	Fire	Earth	Metal	Water
Season	Spring	Early Summer	Late Summer	Fall	Winter
Color	Green	Red	Yellow	White	Black
Zang organs	Liver	Heart	Stomach	Lungs	Kidneys
Fu organs	Gall Bladder	Small Intestine, Sanjiao	Spleen	Large Intestine	Urinary Bladder

The third major Yin and Yan system for health is Jing-Lua, or Meridians.
Jing-Lua Meridians are connected to the *Zang-Fu* where the five elements and Qi flow.

Each organ in the human body contains Yin and Yang, and some organs may have predominant Yin or Yang. For example, the liver is predominantly Yang, while the kidneys are predominantly Yin. Regardless of an organ's predominant state, the body will always have a total sum of Yin and Yang balance.

Our bodies cannot always be in perfect Yin and Yang balance. For example, if we are furious or angry, Yang dominates, and when we are calm and rested, Yin dominates. Emotions must also be balanced, as excess can have a major impact on an organ's health and their Yin and Yang balance. For instance, if one is always angry, the liver is unable to spread Qi adequately. As a result, this will lead to Qi stagnation and problems.

Our seven emotions are stored in the following organs:

Anger -Liver
Joy – Heart
Worry – Spleen
Fear – Kidney
Grief, Sadness – Lung
Worry – Spleen
Shock- Heart and Kidney

It is normal to express the 7 emotions, however; if these emotions become excessive, dominant, and prolong they can damage internal organs and create illness. Emotions are extremely powerful. In Chapter 6 we will discover how they can impact and effect our body and health. Furthermore, in Chapter 12 we will discover and learn how to use emotions correctly in order to enhance balance and health in body, mind and soul. Emotional control and mastery can significantly impact our internal alignment and balance in body, mind, soul, actions and so forth. For example, if one is always joyful, the spirit can be dispersed everywhere. If one has too much anger, the liver is impacted and as a result one may experience headaches, dizziness, high blood pressure, and have stomach and spleen problems. Also, if one has excessive anxiety, this affects Qi in the lungs, and causes short, shallow, and irregular breathing in the short term. In the long run this can affect the lungs organ and large intestine. It is very important that we deal with unresolved emotions, balance and nurture our emotions for health.

In traditional Chinese medicine health is restored when Yin and Yang are balanced and this can be seen in the work of: Traditional Chinese medicine doctors and practitioners, acupuncture, various exercises, herbal remedies, lifestyle and dietary changes. For this reason, the Holistic methodology focuses on starting and ending each session with a calm state of body, mind, and connection to a higher source of power.

In order to keep our Yin and Yang balanced in our body we should avoid consuming heavily processed foods, meditate, eat a balanced macro nutrient diet (carbs, proteins, fats), eat different vegetables and fruits weekly, sleep early, exercise holistically, invest and equally care for: body, emotions, mind, energy and soul.

If one has Yin or Yang deficiency, eating certain foods can help strengthen Yin or Yang. Sample of Foods for Yin and Yang deficiency are:

Yin deficiency foods that help strengthen Yin: eggs, cheese, milk, potatoes, sweet potatoes, squash, string beans, beans, tofu.

Yin deficiency foods to avoid: food and drinks with: sugar, alcohol, caffeine, pungent foods, hot spices, ginger.

Yang deficiency foods that help strengthen Yang: oats, glutinous rice, quinoa, vegetables, kale, onion, ginger and jasmine tea.

Yang deficiency foods to avoid: excess cold or raw food or cold drinks, instead consume lightly steamed foods and warming drinks.

Examples of excess Acute Yin in body are: slow pulse, pale face, no coated tongue, weak blood circulation, lack of appetite, diminutive thirst, light white urine color, clinical neurological disorders, slow or heavy speech, sensitive to cold, lethargy.

Examples of excess Acute Yang in body are: rapid pulse, high blood circulation, yellow coated tongue, reddish face and cheeks, inflammation, strong appetite, high thirst, dark yellow urine, restlessness, anxiety, anger, irritable, loud and rapid speech, sensitive to heat.

Examples of excess Yang and not enough Yin in body are: restlessness, dry skin, scanty urination, constipation, and rapid pulse.

Examples of too much Yin and not enough Yang in body are: feeling cold, not thirsty, low energy, edema, frequent urination, loose stools, and slow pulse.

In the Holistic methodology, Yin and Yang are taught to improve and develop self-awareness and mastery, universal connection and understanding of the cosmos, and to restore health and balance in body, emotions, and mind.

Five Chinese Elements Philosophy

The Five Chinese elements philosophy first appeared in 770 – 476 BC in China, and later was used in: Chinese medicine, philosophy, fengshui, and martial arts.

As previously mentioned, the Five Chinese elements are: metal, wood, fire, water, earth. Each element has its own character, attributes, and can create or destroy another element. All of the elements give birth to how everything is connected, and the entire universal natural phenomena.

In Holistic methodology each element must be mastered, practiced in physical training, Holistic living, and be executed in overall presence. In the Holistic physical movement practice, a student must be strong, alert yet calm, have ability to transform different elements in their practice, expand and grow, and yet act with power and strength, and move like water. The behaviour of the tiger animal is often referred to in the Holistic movement practice to remind students how to act, move, behave, exist, and live. The tiger is further discussed in Chapter 11.

The Five Chinese elements and their attributes are:

Wood: Represents: Growth stage of matter, Flexible, Generating. The negative emotions attached to wood are Anger and Frustration. The positive emotion attached to Wood are Patience.

Fire: Represents: Strength, Determination, Creativity, Expansive. It is Active, Light and Fast. The negative emotions attached to Fire are Anger, Over-Excitation, Impulsive behaviour. The positive emotion attached to Fire are Joy.

Earth: Represents a balance of Yin and Yang. Stabilization, Power, Heaviness, Slow. The negative emotions attached to earth are Anxiety. The positive emotion attached to Earth are Love and Empathy.

Metal: Yin. Represents: Inward motion, Decline of matter, Contracting. It is Hard & Rigid. The negative emotions attached to Metal are Grief and Sadness. The positive emotion attached to metal are Courage.

Water: Yin. Energy is silent, Conserving, Motion is downwards and inwards. The negative emotions attached to Water are Fear, Lack of Will. The positive emotion attached to water are Calmness.

In the Holistic methodology, our movement and techniques honour the 5 Chinese elements. The Holistic exercises represent these concepts, and teaches a student to be mentally and physically: calm, determined, flexible, patient, joyous, loving, empathetic, courageous, stable, have ability to turn within themselves, expand and grow, and yet act like fire, wood, water when needed.

Advanced students master the 5 Chinese elements and are trained to be active, strong, disciplined, flexible, stable, light, and patient in mind and body under all circumstances. Each student is trained to transition between elements in movement, exercise, and life.

Advanced students master various holistic breathing and energy techniques (metal elements) during movement and life. The holistic student must move and act like fire, wood, water, and yet be able to transform to metal and earth when needed. A holistic body has limited or no blockages, natural strength, power, fluidity, flexibility and moves in silence and can rapidly transition to earth or any element when needed.

Applying the 5 Chinese elements in the Holistic movement's physical practice enriches a student's ability to survive real life and out of classroom experiences.

Macrocosm/ Microcosm

The concept of macrocosm and microcosm views the human being as a mini version of the universe. It is one of the most ancient ways in which people have represented existence, and unity between themselves and the greater world. Whatever happens in the macrocosm is reflected in the microcosm. This concept has been seen in Taoism, Buddhism, Upanishads, Spinoza, Schelling, Leibniz, Greek philosophes, and more. The idea originally started in China and declined in the 17th century with the evolution of modern science.

"Therefore, we may consequently state that: this world is indeed a living being endowed with a soul and intelligence…a single visible entity containing all other living entities, which by their nature are all related."

-Plato, Timaeus, 29/30; 4th century B.C.E

Plato developed the macrocosm/ microcosm concept and wrote about it in Timaeus (29d-47e), where he explained that the human being's composition, structure corresponds to the universe's. For example, the human flesh can be seen as earth, the human blood is seen as earths' bodies of waters such as: rivers and sea. Paracelsus said, "Man is a microcosm, or a little world, because he is an extract from all the stars and planets of the whole firmament, from the earth and the elements; and so he is their quintessence." For example, a school is a microcosm of society, what happens in society is mirrored outwards. Another example, one human being is a microcosm of the whole human race.

"As above, so below, as within, so without."

-Alyson Noel

This well known quote translates the Holistic methodology even further by saying that what we see, feel, experience are results of our thoughts. Our universe and our mind are 'As above.' 'So below' is our environment and body. Whatever we think consciously or unconsciously will always return back to us. For example, if we think negative, negative will follow. If we think good, good will follow. If we love ourselves, others will love us.

The human being is a reflection of the universe, and it hosts major and minor divine powers. For this reason, many people feel that they have an inner unknown power. This power does exist, however; it is rarely used or explored. In Kung Fu, we see these super divine powers used through: levitation, iron fists, head, body; chi and energy manipulation, enhanced speed and combat abilities and more. In Yoga we see similar in how a yogi can control and change their heart rate, levitate, open and see through 3rd eye, super senses, extraordinary flexibility and control. In Taoism, movements such as: Tai Chi, meditation, and Qi Qong are focused to improve: alignment, movement, awareness, focus, balance, health, and energy, however; extraordinary powers also rise from the practices. For example, some who practice long to mastery, could gain extraordinary powers to treat and heal people, or manoeuvre and manipulate energy and chi.

In the Holistic methodology, the advanced training, discipline, and knowledge acquired helps one access these superhuman powers. When we understand and re-connect within ourselves, we can understand the entire world and universe. Everything is within us.

"Knowing others is intelligence; knowing yourself is true wisdom. Mastering others is strength; mastering yourself is true power. If you realize that you have enough, you are truly rich."

-Lao Tzu

Ayurveda

Ayurveda, is the traditional Hindu system of the world's oldest holistic healing practices that originated over 3000 years ago from India. It focuses on enriching and balancing health through dosha's and the body, mind and spirit practices.

Ayurvedic therapies are done through: diet, massage, herbal treatment, yoga and yogic breathing.

Within Ayurveda, the Holistic methodology focuses mainly on the dosha's. The dosha's are biological energies found in the human body, mind and spirit and are: Fire (Pitta), Earth (Kapha), Air (Vata).

The common characteristics of each dosha include:

Fire (Pitta): Hot, Sharp, Well Built Body, Intelligent
Earth (Kapha): Steady, Calm, Heavier bone and body structure
Air (Vata): Impulsive, Imagination, Fast, Energetic, smaller and frail bone structure

The Holistic methodology strives to balance the body, emotions, and mind through Holistic movements and breath that are designed to regain dosha balance in private practice or consultations only. Clients who have body, emotions, and mind unbalances can regain balance through various breathing, Holistic and Yoga movement, Ayurvedic massages such as: Abhyanga, Shirodhara, and dietary, lifestyle changes and natural Ayurvedic therapies such as Panchakarma that are complimentary to the Holistic movement.

Holistic Movement & Self- Balance

Self-balance and harmony within oneself are vital in order to happily adjust and continue into the next era. The Yin Yang, 5 Chinese elements philosophy, macrocosm/ microcosm, and Ayurveda concepts are a few of the major integrated philosophies in the Holistic Movement practice.

In the Holistic Movement practice, several beliefs are taught in order to help students reach optimum connection, balance and self-harmony in their life. Many of the Holistic Movement beliefs are shared in Taoism and include:

1. Look within and you will find everything you need
2. Inner cultivation is more important than external development
3. Letting go, and practice of non-attachment
4. Remove labels from self and: things, people, experiences
5. Good is all that flows with the way of the Tao, while evil is anything that puts resistance on your flow from Tao
6. Honor and practice kindness and compassion
7. Be yourself
8. Be humble
9. Change is embraced
10. Practice harmony

The Holistic methodology focuses tremendously on training and disciplining: mind, body, soul to stay and be connected to the divine field. Such training includes training and disciplining: subconscious, thoughts, beliefs, mind, emotions, and internally communicate and activate heart lines of communication within all of these. The quality of our lives depend on how we connect from within, maintain balance, nurture, and access our systems. Our true power, happiness, joy, and health comes from being connected and living in harmony within ourselves and nature.

The Necklace and Bead example reflect how the Holistic methodology honours balance and harmony in its practice. If the string of the necklace is our connection to the divine, each bead is a representation of our systems and self. In the Beaded necklace example, we will only focus on: subconscious, mind, body, and soul since these are the basic fundamentals that are trained in the Holistic methodology. To continue being aligned, and connected to the divine we must equally: train, balance, control, and discipline each bead to stay connected and aligned on the string. Each bead must have equal awareness, advancement, discipline, and training. If one bead is disturbed or missing, our alignment to the universe will be altered. Over time this mis-alignment expands. We are strongest when each bead is balanced, controlled, trained and tuned to the divine's frequency. To achieve this one must train, discipline body, mind, and soul constantly until it becomes as natural as breath. One must master it as a way of life.

Balanced and Connected Beaded Necklace to Divine

Divine Intelligence Field

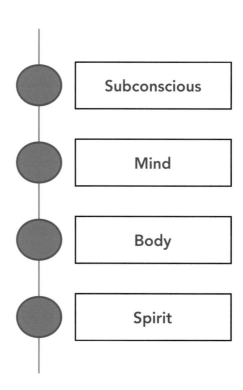

Un- Balanced Dis-connected Beaded Necklace to Divine
(where mind and body are not trained, disciplined, focused)

Divine Intelligence Field

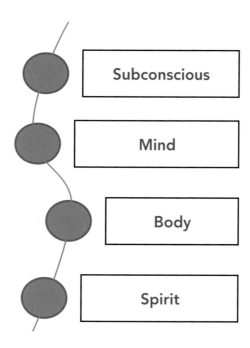

Un-Balanced Dis-connected Beaded Necklace to Divine. (Mind is untrained, unbalanced and in the long run leads to enlarged Mind unbalance).

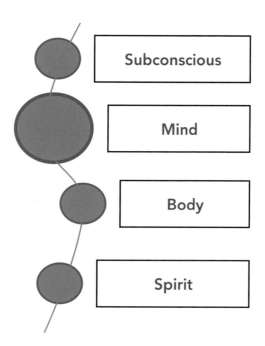

In conclusion, internal discipline, training and balance within our systems is very important as we are constantly attaching ourselves outward rather than inwards. If we are not well balanced, we will attract un-balanced things to our lives and have chaos and instability. It is very important to understand and grasp the Yin Yang, 5 Chinese Elements Philosophy, Macrocosm and Microcosm, Ayurvedic concepts to enrich the quality of our lives, regain health and create unity with everything around us. Once we understand and implement the concepts, our lives will be dramatically balanced and enhanced.

Vesica Pisces

In the Holistic methodology, the Vesica Pisces concept is very important to understand because its' sacred symbol is the birth shape of very complex geometry that surrounds us everywhere. We must learn to see beyond our eyes, and realize that our life is an illusion, as we will see in Chapter 4, and we can re-create it.

The Vesica Pisces is the womb of the universe that consists of two circles that overlap with one another. The first circle is the basis of all fixed entities, including the self, consciousness, and existence. It gives birth to the entire universe. Its' circular form has no boundaries, definitions, size, and is the only fixed thing that can emerge from formless infinity. In the early cultures, God was symbolized as a circle, as being eternal. In the first circle, God, the Observer is male in the spiritual world.

The second circle symbolizes the start of duality, and is the Goddess, the observed in the physical world.

Vesica Pisces

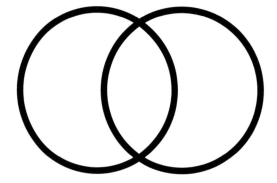

The design of the Vesica Pisces goes back thousands of years preceding major religions, and shows the Flower of Life, and Tree of life. Its' shape was formed first in nature, and is seen in artwork from Christ, Buddha, Medieval churches, and even presently in modern architecture and the Channel Coco Logo. Everything that exists emerged from this shape. It represents expansion, creation, and birth.

If a third circle is added to the Vesica we see Trinity which is: father, son, spirit all connected to the Divine and everything around us.

Trinity

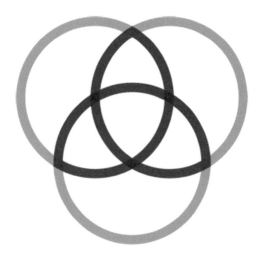

If the Vesica pattern is replicated we see the Flower of life, an ancient symbol that has been seen in many ancient icons, art, and temples. It represents the cycle of creation, and how everything started from a singular source. The Flower of life is the foundation of geometry, music, and divine proportions. The first circle is perceived where life began, and is the blueprint of all life that contains all basic patterns around us. It signifies that everything is connected to the geometric plan by the one divine source. Every structure in life is following this plan. In the Holistic methodology, this is important to understand because we must know the design of our external universe and the world we also live in. We must also reflect on ancestral knowledge, and history to understand our external world.

Flower Of Life

In the Flower of life, five shapes are seen and exist in all building blocks of life. These shapes are: the tetrahedron, cube, octahedron, dodecahedron, and icosahedron. These shapes are found in: chakras, minerals, sound, language, music and more. They are everywhere.

The Flower of life is seen in the: Forbidden City Of China, Buddhist temples in India and Japan, in carving in Assyria, Turkey, and on the Temple Of Osiris in Abydos in Egypt.

Exercise: Take a piece of any cloth, napkin, towel, home decorations, make up pallet, a lettuce leaf, broccoli, or a carrot. Carefully exam all of the shapes, patterns, designs that are seen and repeated to create its form.

From the exercise, you will notice that we and everything around us and within us are all based on repetitive shapes and patterns. In the advanced Holistic movement training, students grasp and understand the Vesica Pisces concept to practice energy manipulation, energy fields, eye projection, healing, and more. This is one of the most advanced concepts that is presented only to students that have proven their loyalty and mastery of the Holistic methodology. It may take a student around 12 years of Holistic movement practices, knowledge, and training to reach this level.

In conclusion, our universe has a super consciousness that is incredibly sophisticated. Our world seems more like a stimulated patterned environment, in which our conscious makes it seem real. However; everything in the universe is geometric, and our understanding of patterns can enrich our practices in visualization, meditation, and overall how the world and universe works.

Discipline

To know, train, and master the body, mind, soul is not enough, we must practice self-discipline. Discipline is extremely important in the Holistic methodology, as nothing can be done without it.

In the Holistic methodology, training and discipline at later stages continues regardless of our: emotions, thoughts, feelings, weather, social status, income, and environment. This state of discipline comes over consistency, repetition, and guidance. Most people may quickly begin to engage in a sport, activity, or study and then suddenly drop out. In the Holistic methodology, discipline defines a student's success. Discipline is a way of life that is grown and rooted within oneself.

Discipline gives one: structure, self-control, and stability. As we saw in the Yin and Yang concept, if the world is chaotic, we must practice more self-discipline or self- order to have balance. If our world is too strict, then we most practice free movement, expression to keep balance. Self-discipline is important to overcome: addictions, smoking, negative behaviour/habits, eating disorders, lack of movement, and to inspire change within ourselves. Discipline is the prescription for our thoughts, emotions, actions, and wandering mind. The act of self-discipline is needed to: improve, grow, and acquire new skills.

The Holistic Movement, is a discipline in body, emotions, and mind. It teaches us how to master and control our entire self. To thrive in discipline, we must know our: weaknesses and change them to our strengths. We must possess an inner will power, as taught in Chapter 1. We must be willing to let go of the old: thoughts, emotions, behaviour, or habits in order to create space for the new. Discipline has the power to dissolve inner conflict and dispute, and create a strong self. It is very important to understand that true discipline takes time, consistency, and repetition. Once it is achieved, you can gain: control, mental clarity, emotional balance, behaviour, confidence, progress, and a strong inner self connection to combat all of life's challenges.

As we previously learnt in the Life Maze concept, our entire body and mind system can be viewed as being a class room filled with a united color of students from all systems. Our mind is one classroom that has a mix of: thought students, belief students, emotion students, logic and cognitive students. Our body is another classroom that possess all of our bodily part students. For example, our arm, finger, torso, neck, back, leg, head and so forth are each a student. Within those students other smaller students may exist. For example, our hand is a student, that is connected or possesses 5 finger students. Discipline must constantly exist in each student and classroom for success and self-mastery. We must learn to control our entire classroom daily. If we can hear our students breathe, we can know their entire life story. Breath and its discipline are very important. Our breath should be trained to be quiet when we run or train rather than loud and irregular. Students without discipline will have difficulty to thrive.

Allow us to conceptualize the concept of student, classroom and discipline further. For example, a new rule has now been announced in the mind classroom. Your new waking up time will be at 5 am. As soon as this message is announced, all of the emotion, thoughts, beliefs and other systems may start jumping and say, "This is not fair, why me, this is impossible, I don't want this, I will do anything to sleep at my old regular hours etc…" All kinds of emotions, thoughts, and beliefs may start to erupt. This is a very normal reaction, however; with a truly well disciplined student, acceptance of something that is good for one should be embraced rather than accepting change with resistance. Each student should work together calmly to embrace the new 5 am wake up rule. Discipline creates and empowers change, otherwise we will always be subject to return to our old self and patterns of thought and behaviour. For change to be life long, each student must be trained, disciplined, and live on the same frequency and vision.

"Discipline should become as natural as breath."

-Julie Rammal

The first act of discipline in the Holistic methodology was described in Chapter One, the belief that you have the power to change. This belief is imprinted in one's mind so that any rising or crossing negative belief will be eliminated. The power of the new belief is more disciplined, trained, and consumed in belief that the old belief has no room to stay. The new belief becomes the winner. The belief that one has the power to change is repetitively believed, repeated with discipline, and rewired in the mind in delta frequency so change can follow. A belief alone is not enough, we must have disciplined thought. Even though our beliefs may change in our life, there are fundamental beliefs of being that do not change. For example: I believe I have an inner power. The act and determination of discipline is the mother of all thoughts and actions that builds success.

"Without self- discipline, success is impossible. Period."
-Lou Holtz

In summary, the Holistic methodology and its disciplinary approach is a way of life. Without discipline one cannot achieve proper evolvement and self-fulfilment to connect deeper within and outside of oneself. The awareness, precision, coordination, focus, inner and outer connection, and movements help one navigate the: body, mind, and all within to regain inner harmony.

CHAPTER 3:

History & Future Of The Human Specie & Sport

The history of everything in and out of our earth shows us that the human specie is de-attaching from being human like, and evolving or de-evolving in a new era of change. We must learn and reflect on history to understand where we are presently at, and where we are heading to, as a human specie.

The origin of the universe is the origin of everything. To know ourselves, we must know the world within to understand the world outside of ourselves. To start from the root of where we are today, and where we are heading, we must reflect back and understand the: akashic field, birth of the universe, earth, evolution of the human specie and the future human specie to rise.

Akashic Field

During the creation of Earth, universe, stars, and galaxies, everything was believed to have been created in the Akashic Field. This field is believed to hold all the information, past, present, and future memory.

In Hindu, it is referred to as Akasha, meaning space or ether. The Akashic field can be thought of as a library containing all references and information from our universe. Ervin Laszlo was a Hungarian philosopher of science, and he believed that the universe consists of energy and information. This contradicts previous conceptions that the universe was believed to be made up of only matter and space.

All of the information from experiences, and feelings are vibrationally absorbed into our chakras, which is later transferred to the Akashic records. We can gain access to this field through holistic energy sessions, meditation, energy chakra work, reiki, shamanic therapies, or opening the 8th chakra.

When we mediate, let go of ego, re-connect, and enter an altered state of consciousness we can gain access to this field. Our questions are answered, and we may have better directions of where and what to do in our lives. Through practice one awakens dormant areas in their self, and can also gain super natural abilities such as: healing powers, intuition, extra sensory awareness, and physic abilities.

Many historical leaders, artists, physics, poets, influencers have accessed this field to gain insight, knowledge, vision of changing history and lives of others. I have created my DVD: "In Light of Change" through accessing the field, in which I have shared all of the information, messages and insights with humanity.

In conclusion, the Akashic field can be used to download information, answers, and to connect further with an unlimited library of information from past, present, and future. The Holistic Movement presents access to this field through Holistic energy and meditations that produce remarkable results in body, mind, and soul.

Big Bang

Stephen Hawkins created the Big Bang theory and shared that: with the Big Bang all: space, time, matter, and energy were created. Before the Big Bang, there was nothing. This enormous explosion threw matter in all directions and caused space to expand. As the Universe cooled, galaxies, stars, planets, and earth were formed with the material in the universe. Earth was created around 4.6 billion years ago. Helium is thought to be the first element that was created in the universe, followed by Hydrogen. Other elements were later created and became the building blocks of life. Upon that time, the sound Om vibrated in the universe. The sound and vibration of Om is at a 432 Hz, which is same frequency found in everything in nature. If chanted, the primordial sound Om tunes us back to everything on Earth and in our universe.

Origins of Life

We do not know how the origins of life actually formed on Earth, as scientists, and religions each have their own theories and beliefs. One theory explains that the first molecules of life may have met on clay, other theories state that life started from water and deep sea vents, or life started from outside of earth. In either case wherever life began, we know for a fact that, billions of years ago, microbial life forms existed. These microbial life forms could survive extreme high and low temperature and pressure and conditions, and did not have a nucleus. Later on, oxygen started to form on earth, creating a thick ozone layer, and other forms of life died and formed. As a result, life started to grow on land. There were a combination of fishes who adapted to land and began adapting to what became known as amphibians. With time, during the Age of the Amphibians, weather changed, and reptiles were formed. As the temperature later warmed, dinosaurs were formed and lived on a super continent around 160 million years ago. As plate tectonics occurred dinosaurs were drifted apart, and are believed to have become extinct by an asteroid that hit earth around 65 millions years ago. **Internal and external movement gave life to every specie, plant, and animals.**

Apes are believed to have existed around 55 million years ago in Africa. As time passed, green grass and trees were seen in the Sahara allowing apes to move to new food sources. **The first movement that the human specie can connect with today is the sport of walking with two legs, and using their hands. As the apes, used their hands, walked on two legs, their brain sizes also began to increase. Evolution and movement changed their history and ours by expanding our function of our body and minds. They started to master their body through hand use and created stone tools.** Their communication and language were not like the human being language used today. As their brain sizes increased, around 2.5 million years ago some left Africa. **Their movements, were to run, crawl, throw and grab, balance, walk, jump, hunt, and to survive in their environments. Therefore, we can see an enormous connection between movement and the actions to survive in all of history.** However, around 2 million years ago, some of those who left Africa eventually became extinct. Approximately, 1.8 million years ago, the homo erectus specie lived. They were the first hunter and gatherers. Until today, this skill of gathering things still exists within our specie. We are always gathering food, items, objects etc… Around 500,000 years ago they could build shelters, and 400,000 years ago tools were being created. Roughly 230,000 years ago, Neanderthals lived, and became extinct when the homo sapien specie was created 195,000 years ago. Approximately 170,000 years ago the Mitochondrial Eve lived, known as the mother to all human species or Eve. From their human beings developed an ability to speak, make jewellery, had burial ceremonies, and later life evolved to different periods such as the: stone age, ancient period, middle ages, and modern, agriculture, industrial era etc…**The movements of the human specie changed tremendously in these eras: from working close to nature with their hands to using their body and mind to survive.** There was also a very similar hominid specie that is called *Homo Apriliensis, and it resembled the human specie however it had a tail. The tail is believed to help with balance.* British paleoanthropologist John Bennett discovered this specie in fossil form on 1st April 2019 and stated, "This could be the most significant discovery in human origins research in 100 years!" The body was discovered in a cave in Siberia, and showed DNA traces from the Denisovans and Homo sapiens. As a result, these three species were believed to have had reproduced at some point. We as modern humans still possess remaining traits such as: wisdom teeth, appendix, and the coccyx. This tail is seen today in human embryos in the first four weeks. As the embryo develops, the tail is absorbed in the growing coccyx and body, however; our tailbone still remains.

As the human specie continued to develop through mind, the tail eventually vanished and this specie was extinct. As the Homo Sapien, or human specie advanced with their use of hands, they expanded their brain capacity. With time, they created and became dependent on equipment and technology to clean their: clothes, hunt, cook, communicate, work, commute etc... With time, our dependency on technology increased and will continue to increase. Due to the technological changes, our bodies have become weaker, and continue to lose their natural means of movement and existence. During the rapid evolution and birth of technology, the human specie has not correctly adapted or survived the transition to the new technological decades. Our bodies have taken thousands of years to develop, and within less than 200 years we have advanced everything in our world, however; our bodies have not evolved as quickly. As a result, we see dis-harmony in our body, emotions, and mind. For example, there is a significant increase in pain, injuries, illnesses, obesity, eating disorders, weakness, joint problems, etc. Many of the new symptoms are mainly attributed to our body's inability to rapidly catch up with the rapid changes that have taken place, such as in our surrounding environment and in our way of living. The Holistic movement and methodology facilitates the human body, emotions, and mind to adapt to the current and future era.

Modern Human Interconnected To Multiple Devices and Technology

Evolution Of The Human Specie

The only thing that joins our physical state with our ancestors is our body and initiation and act of movement. Today, many of us have forgotten the primordial means to: eat, sleep, move and exercise, breathe, think, survive and exist, and are constantly living anxiety and stress. Our minds and body get anxious and stressful, because they are not ready for where we are today. We must re-connect inside and outside of ourselves, and to everything above us. It is important to rebuild our body, heart and mind connection in order to enhance our lives today and in the future. We must re-connect to remember the history of the human specie, and ignite our powers of being human. A human being is supposed to be love, follow the divine laws, remain connected and grounded to nature and the universe, and everything will flow in harmony. The Holistic movement enhances the natural flow of life in and outside of ourselves.

In the Holistic methodology it is emphasized that one must dig within to get the external world they desire. It is very important to know oneself in and out. One of the most valuable assets that humans still have are their heart power and ability to feel and have emotions. As such, the human heart is the only organ that can communicate directly with the divine. Throughout history, the heart was the first and foremost dominant part of our body, and then the mind advanced with the technological revolution. Today, our hearts and minds should be exercised more, and filled with love and positivity.

Not all humans are in the same level of evolution, and during our primal to complex evolution very few of us understood the super human and natural powers that we possess. Very few of us knew how to train the: body, the mind, subconscious, thoughts, beliefs, emotions, protect our soul, and to connect to our universal source. Those who did, thrived and changed, while others must be gently awaken to know their precious value, body, mind, and self. To understand, control, discipline, self-communicate, know and master ourselves, in body and mind together, these are the secrets to spark our powers to surpass the challenges in the next era. A huge awakening is beginning to occur, and the Holistic methodology guides those to discover their awakened self, powers, and ignite them beyond imagination.

Current Human Movement

Today, the human specie has been vacuumed physically, mentally, and emotionally into a wave of concepts, trends, materialism and everything that is not truly human.

It is important that we re-connect to the practice of genuine sports for the current and future generations. Genuine movement is free in motion, and was our main part of survival before the birth of our minds. Today, as our minds have grown and expanded, movement seems complex and destructed. We see applications to train our: butt, abs, or triceps, however; this is not sport. Sport is body, mind, and spirit working together to perform a sport with discipline. The Holistic methodology believes in training the entire system as one and maintaining its internal and external alignment with the divine.

The human body is facing an epidemic and crisis, in which we are losing touch with our body, and ourselves. Despite rapid technological evolution, we must honour the history of the body, and understand that our body is not ready for such changes. Our body only understands natural movements such as: dance, walking, running, hiking, rolling over, crawling, squatting, gymnastics, martial arts, tai chi etc…These are natural movements that our body recognizes. According to ancestral books and knowledge, our bodies are made to last 900 years. However, today our bodies are breaking down in our 30's and in our 70's and 80's the majority are not in splendid shape. It is important that we live within our bodies, and understand its' language.

The Holistic methodology understands the body, and trains it with the natural body code of movement. It is believed that movement is natural and free in motion, and should serve the body, mind and spirit. It should be: joyous, natural, healing, therapeutic, energized, and youthful in the Holistic modality. The Holistic methodology trains and disciplines the: body, mind, and spirit equally together. Movement is the one thing that we share with our ancestors millions of years ago, and proper natural movement is what the body should exercise. Allow us to re-attach back to this natural skill to enhance the lives of all humans. We should treat our bodies as a historical temple filled with incredible power and wisdom, rather than a tool or device controlled by gadgets and conscious mind. The Holistic Movement will re-connect your body, mind, soul, and awaken your entire system and connection to the universe for an abundance of joy, health, energy, and youthfulness.

To be connected, we must master our inner inventory of: heart, body, subconscious, thought, belief, energy and vibration, mind, and spirit to enrich our lives. The Holistic methodology uncovers and reveals the secrets to understanding and training our body, mind, and spirit to bring proper internal balance, control, discipline and equilibrium within and outside of ourselves.

In conclusion, when we look at the history of movement, movement was meant for survival and ceremony. Movement was beautiful, free, and natural. It existed in various forms such as: dancing, walking, running, hiking, spear throwing, balancing, catching, grabbing, and fighting. Today we must honor and love our body, treat it as a temple, and move freely to improve our body, mind health, and connection to the universe.

Future Human Being

The future human specie will be more and more connected internally and externally to technology if the human specie is not awakened to take control and a stance over their body mind and spirit.

Every specie is constantly evolving or devolving to extinction. We are predicted to emerge as a distinct homo sapien specie of the hominid, great apes, family with the use of technology. Scientists predict that we may have stopped evolving as technology continues to increase. If our evolution has stopped, humans may rise to become a new specie that is half human and half machine with technology flowing within us.

The future of the human specie may take three major directions. The first is, we only change and remain as we are with new races emerging and minor new technological tweaks within us. The second, a new human specie completely evolves. Thirdly, machines and human brains are interconnected to produce intelligence. This will be the death of the human specie, and the mark of a new artificially intelligent specie, where everything will be computerized, controlled, and digitalized.

A few predictions that will continue to evolve in the medical field are: nanobots and gene therapy. Nanobots are mini robots that are only 50-100 nm wide, and will be increasingly used around our body to enhance our natural abilities, kill cancer, and disease. In addition, the rise of gene therapy and modification will continue. Genes can be modified in the entire human as a whole or for organs. The rise of artificial intelligence will continue to increase and govern our lives, however; the ability for it to over take a human depends on how awakened, and receptive the human specie is. Artificial intelligence should not interfere in our natural movements or lives, as it should be used only to improve our lives without over consuming us.

In the future, we will have more robots around us that will replace our injured limbs, and motivate us to perform certain tasks. This robotic growth may rise to control our entire being by co-existing with our brain.

Overall, the human being and their human life is predicted to shrink by natural causes or self- destruction. Our brains are shrinking, rather than growing as we have seen in our ancestors. No one knows exactly where we might evolve to become. However; we can change history with our decisions, awakening and using our internal power systems, and engaging with the Holistic Movement to re-connect in body, mind, and soul to ourselves and the universe.

Future Robotic Human

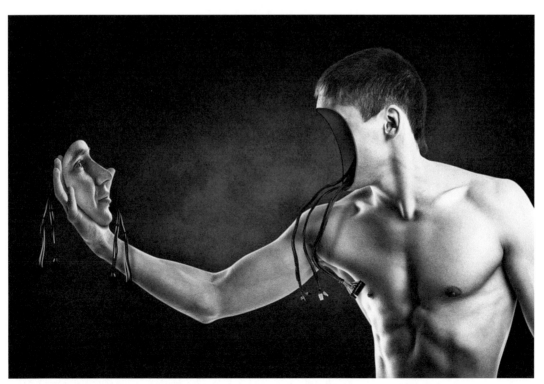

Woman Robot

Future Ant Robot Used To Rebalance Ecosystem

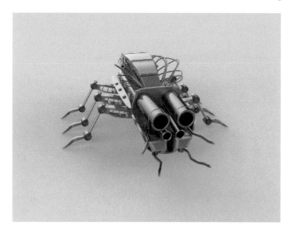

Artificial Spider

Sport

In the Holistic movement, sport requires body and mind connection, inner communication, discipline, training and control to engage in a profound skilful athletic activity.

The World Sports Encyclopaedia (2003), has recorded there are 8000 indigenous sports and sporting games. From 8000, only 200 of them have international recognition.

The birth of sports and competitions most probably started during the Stone Age period. Cave drawings have shown images of: wrestling, sprinting, and archery. In addition, around 3000 years ago, towards the end of the 6th century BC, there were four major sporting events that took place. The Olympic Games at Olympia was the most well known sporting event. In 776 B.C, the first written record recorded Corobeus winning a 192 meter footrace. Other ancient games included: running, long jump, shot put, javelin, boxing, pankration and horse-racing events. Wrestling, the oldest form of combat was mentioned in the Bible, and ancient Indian vedas. This re-emphasizes that the skill of running, and combat was heavily used to survive and entertain throughout movements history.

Dancing, walking, jumping, and running are our joint movements that unites us to our ancestors. It is the language that our body understands, and the base movements that the Holistic methodology practices. All other sport skills were acquired through various sport movements such as: martial arts, specific dance methods, gymnastics, boxing, equestrian, discus, javelin, fighting, MMA, Yoga, Pilates, Aerobics etc…

The first modern sports schools were created in Moscow and other cities in the USSR. These schools gave birth to famous Olympic athletes. Later on, similar sport schools and systems were adopted in other countries such as China. In 1951, the USSR joined the International Olympic Committee, and from there new specialized youth schools expanded under the Olympic Reserve. Each student was trained and disciplined to perform their best in the Olympic Games. Afterwards, new sport disciplines and schools expanded worldwide, and sports practices and methodologies spread to private businesses, studios, and so forth.

In conclusion, from history, many life forms were created, destroyed, evolved but the one thing that every creature, human did was move, and movement meant survival. Today, movement is being re-taught. There are gym rules on how to move, and movement seems to be a vanishing luxury item in our lives. For the majority of us, our movements are decreasing in range of motion, distance and frequency, and for many of us moving has become painful. As we are becoming more dependent on technology, we are losing the essence of movement and sport. Today, we have forgotten how to move, and rely on: applications, gadgets, pills, exercises to move or motivate us to move. We must remember the only language that our body understands is free and natural movement.

The Holistic methodology is an educational discipline in sport that offers the methods to help us re-connect, move, train, discipline, and align: our body, mind, and soul within and outside of ourselves to the universe.

Holistic Body, Julie Rammal, Founder Of Holistic Movement

Holistic Body, Julie Rammal, Founder Of Holistic Movement

Chapter 4:

Transformation Secrets in Our World

In Chapter 2, we learnt that we are born into a Life Maze, and within one's maze it is important to know oneself, the world, one's inner gifts, and to have a clear vision to reach the end of one's maze. In this chapter, we will reveal the secrets to excel in the maze, uplift and transform body, mind, soul, and decode the code of the universe.

As we may recall from Chapter 1, change should be embraced. The Holistic Movement provides an open door to all who want to empower and adapt to the current and future changes in oneself and the world. Change may not always be easy, however; once it is initiated change can bring incredible things to your life. The real change must come from within oneself. We do not need to force change, however; we must believe we can change. The thought alone will attract change to manifest at the divine time. The rate of change can be excelled when our desire to change is greater than where we stand. If we have a strong desire, decision, and a vision of the changes we want to embrace, the rate of change can be outstanding. Life should be happy, joyous, fun, creative, positive and fulfilling with amazing things, and if it is not then you must dig within to initiate the external change. When we reconnect to our inner self, we can better understand the world we live in, and transform harmoniously within the code of the universe and Holistic methodology.

Code Of The Universe

Everything in and around our life has codes. The key to understanding the code of the universe lies in understanding ourselves, the language of the universe, lost ancient knowledge, the field of energy, vibration, karma, and patterned energy. To create our brilliant worlds' we must find our place on earth, the universe, our purpose, vision, reflect on ancient knowledge, and learn the language of the divine universe.

Recently, western science is now beginning to understand and dig deeper that everything is connected to a vast field of energy. The human being comes from the same particles that existed in the Big Bang! It is only our conscious minds that make reality appear the way it is, however; as the father of quantum physics, Max Planck said in the late 1990's that "The matter that we see in our world does not exist." Underneath our mind is a field where all matter is connected. Our ancient ancestors detected, accessed and used this field. Shamanism is one example of indigenous native people from Siberia and central Asia who transcended healing energies by connecting to a higher spirit world. This practice originated over 5000 years ago and focuses on removing, healing blockages, and reuniting missing pieces of the soul. The Holistic healing sessions also access and use this beautiful field. Our ancestors were very in tune with energy and its field because they were connected harmoniously with nature. They did not have the technological distractions that we have today, and wore natural clothes from animals, walked barefoot, slept at sunset, and woke up at sunrise. Their inner cycles were in tune with their environmental cycles of nature.

Today, we must re-attach ourselves back to nature, and when possible, one should walk barefoot, and be in touch with earth's soil, plants, flowers, animals and everything that naturally exists in our world. Grounding ourselves back to earth has immense benefits that neutralizes free radicals, improve immunity, sleep, decrease inflammation, stress, infection, and cell damage.

Science has also recently accepted that everything including our: emotions, beliefs, thoughts have an effect on our bodies, our lives, and on this greater scale field that envelopes our world. Science has now accepted that we live in a field where everything is mirrored back to us, or holographic. In a hologram, every piece of something mirrors the entire something. In other words, everything from galaxies, stars to the tiniest atom is all included in the universal hologram. What we bring inside of us becomes our reality. We can create our own positive fields of energy and changes by engaging in the Holistic methodology, prayer, empowering and positive thoughts and beliefs, and love which all have a beautiful effect on our frequencies.

Vibration

Everything in our universe, nature, earth, and matter is constantly vibrating at a certain frequency. Sound and thoughts are a vibration. Our thoughts vibrate and match other vibrations which later become our reality. We can change our vibration by activating our brain cells to activate our body, surround ourselves with positive vibes, being kind, grateful, exercise, re-connect with nature, and have conscious awareness of what we think, say, and feel.

"Everything in Life is Vibration"
– Albert Einstein

Karma

Karma is the law of the Spiritual World that functions like a boomerang. In Sanskrit, karma means action, and it refers to the spiritual principle of cause and effect. It is comparable to Newton's law that 'every action must have a reaction.' Through our words, thoughts, and actions we initiate a force that will return back to us. This force may be returned modified, but it is difficult to avoid. One example of Karma is, if you steal something from someone, this action will get stored in your: mind, body, soul or genes, and will also be stored in the person's soul who you stole from. This theft action is uploaded to the universe or Akashic records, and later on as planets and constellations move, it is re downloaded to you in similar or modified form. This is karma. Therefore, one must be very careful of their thoughts, beliefs, and actions. Through the law of forgiveness, we can sometimes dissolve karma. This only may work if we truly feel the other soul's pain, guilt, and feel sorry for the pain and loss that the other soul felt. From there, we can ask their soul for forgiveness. Karma can take years to hundreds of years to forgive. The universe is always seeking compassionate and humane beings.

Energy, Fractals, Maya

In 1975 scientists discovered that fractal patterns exist and repeat themselves everywhere and in everything around us. These patterns repeat in a recursive code on different scales, and can be seen all over in nature, and the universe. Examples of fractals are seen in: leaves, apples, mountains, fruits, trees, snowflakes, clouds, and even throughout our circulatory system.

Within all of this patterned energy lies living information. Allow us to scan how electrons move around the nucleus of an atom. This same pattern of movement is seen in how the moon moves around Earth, or how planets are moving around the sun and so forth. All patterns are made from a recursive code that repeats itself over and over again on various different scales. These re-occurring patterns is what makes everything in life run. The duration of this pattern will continue until it reaches its limit of complexity, or time. For this exact reason, many ancients, and now modern science believe we are living in a stimulation. Everything we see appears only because of our conscious mind. However, the reality is that it doesn't really exist as we perceive it to be. Scientists have also discovered that this coded, repeated pattern directs the cells of our body, the atoms of physical matter, and how they are combined to create the images we see in the world. In Hindu philosophy this stimulation was referred to as Maya, or illusion or deception. Interestingly, they believed that only with the act of goodness, can one gain and develop wisdom to see things in the real perspective. In addition, Maya or illusion, must be overcome to free the soul from karma. In Buddhism and Sikhism there are similar conceptions of Maya or illusion. In very early Vedic mythology, Maya or illusion was seen as the deities, or Gods power to create and sustain the universe. Afterwards, the Upanishads, from the school of Advaita Vedanta, believed that Maya or illusion is connected to a greater cosmic power. They called it Braham. It has been long believed that we are living in an illusion, and that present things are not really present the way we think they are. It is our conscious mind that perceives it. For instance, if we did not have a mind, we might perceive the world in a different state such as: imaginative or hallucinated. Our world is changing according to what our conscious mind perceives, and what we think and believe. For example, when we sleep, our entire world is silent, mysterious and a completely different world. When we wake up our world is seen through our conscious minds. Or, if we are having a bad day, and do a head stand, our world looks different when we are upside down.

"Pure consciousness is the only reality. Physical universe is virtual reality."
-Braham Satya Jagat Mithya

In Hindu teachings, it is believed that all physical matter is a combination of things that maintain its current state. If we change one of those things, then the object becomes something else. Therefore, what we consider to be real is only a constrained sense and perspective. In Hindu 'Prakriti, the universal mother is the cause of all manifestation and movement in the universe and its' consciousness. The universal mother, 'Prakriti,' also has ''Kshetra," which are field forces that exist behind all activity and movement that takes place in the universe.

Our illusive world has limits depending on the duration of the stimulation, and how large the universe is. When we reflect on our daily lives, we lived a patterned life. This pattern cycle is seen in our daily routine, relationship, work cycles etc…Many people may be looking for change, and think by re-locating a change or shift in their life may happen. However, this is not how it necessarily works. Patterns are imprinted in our system, and by re-locating those same patterns still exist, and will attract the same situations or experiences. We are living fractal patterns in our emotions, relationships and in our biological system because the energy of power stimulation is governed by the fractal code.

"Insanity: doing the same thing over and over again, and expecting different results."
-Albert Einstein

To change this pattern, we must change one variable, value, and truly stick to it. For example, we can shift one thought, feeling, habit, belief, action, or be more grateful. As a result, new patterns will rise and repeat repetitively again. Our experience is following the code of information that governs our entire stimulation. To change anything in our life, it is important to understand the code of the universe, fractal pattern codes, and tune into our inner inventory. The universe only understands one language, emotion and feelings through the heart. Love, is the strongest emotion that projects the largest field. We can change our fractal patterns and experiences by truly speaking from our hearts in changing one variable such as: value, belief, action and so forth.

Belief

The power of belief creates our reality, and can change matter. Beliefs give birth to our reality, and our brain neurons appear very similar to the strands of the universe. It is through our beliefs and thoughts we can create our reality.

Today, most of us are living other people's beliefs, because up until the age of 7 years old, our friends, family, and environment would transfer and implant their beliefs into our subconscious mind. As a result, we are only living other people's programs. The Holistic methodology helps re-program our mind to create our own personalized life.

As we previously learnt, we are made of quantum energy, and it is only our consciousness that holds our entire self together. In 2018 Max Planck, who won the noble prize, said that everything in our world does not exist the way we think it does. He said, "Our beliefs, translate invisible energy back to the universe. If we want to change the stuff, we must change the energy that the stuff exists or lives in." Einstein said, "The field that connects everything together is the governing agency of the particle." In other words, the magnetic and electric field determines the atom's behaviour. An atom can be changed if one of the fields is changed.

Humans are reality makers that can only make what they believe through use of emotion through their hearts. If we do not feel, and have emotion in our belief then our belief will never reap.

Mahayana Buddhism teaches us that we create that "something" through the force of consciousness and awareness. In the teachings, "It's believed that reality can exist only where our mind creates a focus" and "observation is an act of creation, and that consciousness is doing the creating." This is why in the Holistic methodology awareness, connection, emotion, meditation, discipline and focus are very important principles to change and rewire the mind. Our positive feelings like: gratitude, love, compassion, kindness have the power to even change our DNA. We must put positive emotions such as: peace, gratitude, positivity, and joy to initiate healing in our bodies. Through our hearts, we can create the feeling, and re-affirm it through our thoughts and beliefs, and live as if the belief or thought has actually already happened. Through this method change is guaranteed if practiced genuinely. You can repeat to yourself "It has already happened," and remember to: act, think, and be the belief that you believe is to come. The field mirrors the now moment so what we choose to experience in our lives we must feel in our hearts as if it has happened.

The ancient traditions believed in this spiritual mystery, and they knew that whatever we absorb in our mind triggers a process inside our body. This movement interacts with the divine field and forces that affects our physical world. Allow us to reflect on major events that have happened such as 9-11. During the 9-11 event, scientists detected a shift in consciousness on September 10, and later 9-11 occurred. Whatever the human consciousness focuses on, will create the reality. Imagine that every time you go to work, you pass by and look at the same barber shop every time for 7 days in a row. As your conscious mind focuses on the barber shop, the probability of you entering and getting a haircut will be very high. Lastly, another example of focus and fields of energy is the actualization of a workshop that I had to give in the heart of Beirut, during a climax hour, in the middle of the intense Lebanese 2019-2020 revolution. The workshop was a self-transformation workshop that was schedule to start at 6 pm, which was the climax hour for protests as protestors finished work. Through the power of my mind, visualization, I created the field that I had desired to see in order for the workshop to take place. This is called field manipulation, a very advance practice in the holistic methodology. The workshop was extremely successful, overbooked, and started exactly at 6 pm. I was able to pause the external events by creating the field I had desired. As soon as the workshop finished, the rise of the protests immensely regrouped suddenly. This shows us the power of our self, and how we can truly create and change things in our lives. Videos of this workshop can be seen on the Holistic Movement website, www.holisticmovement.co

The Chi, or energy is well mastered in the Holistic methodology and advance martial art students. In the Holistic methodology, advanced students are taught how to use energy and manipulate energy and fields through various techniques such as Eye Projection. Today and in the future, people, science and medicine may not always know or have the answers and remedies for outbreaks, pandemics, suffering, and more. Hopefully in the future, the Holistic practice of field and energy manipulation may be used to heighten healing, remedies for pandemics, outbreaks, spread love, peace and more.

Your Heart

Our heart is alive, and it has no judgement, ego, fear, and is more intelligent than our brain.

It has around 40,000 neurons, the same as the brain, and it emits 5 times more electromagnetic or energy than our brain's. Our heart also forms its own neural pathways just like the brain. The electromagnetic field of your heart extends for several feet in all directions outside of your body, and when we pray from our heart this field is extended. If you feel positive emotion, it will make your entire body feel good, energetic, and affect your health. The heart can spread positivity, love, happiness, care, appreciation to everything inside and around us. As a result, it changes the pattern of activity in the nervous system, boosts immunity, and reduces stress. It is important to live from your heart space, as it's a very powerful powerhouse that emits positive messages and energy.

One should create: thoughts, feelings, emotions, beliefs, compassion and practice forgiveness. When we generate those feelings, we increase our electromagnetic fields from our heart centre. We are also living by the code of the universe. *All of our feelings are uploaded to the universal field, and are downloaded back to us as events.* Our feelings speak to the higher energy or universe. When something happens in this field, the effects can be widely felt.

"Out beyond the ideas of wrong doing and right doing, there is a field I will meet you there."

-Rumi

Rumi explains in this no ego and no judgement field, miracles and healing can exist. However; it must all start from our hearts. In Cherokee traditions, they say "Single eye of the heart that sees what is." The heart sees what is, without judgement, bias, ego or fear. Within that seeing you can create peace, and healing in your space. If our hearts have: compassion, gratitude, forgiveness, transformation will happen. It is important that we enter and access our universal heart, and understand that compassion is the only force that connects everything together in our universe.

Our heart is our golden tool, that can communicate with the divine. The divine understands the frequencies and feelings that are released from your heart. When we ask from our heart, we must feel as though it happened in order to manifest what you have asked for. We should ask without judgement, ego, fear, and let our heart genuinely connect to the divine. Once we ask, feel, and act that change, change will happen. You can speak from your heart by saying, "Please let there be healing, please let there be sun, please let my soulmate come to my life …" but it is important to feel what you are asking for. The divine is very generous and giving to those who open their hearts.

The power and connection of feeling can change our world when it comes from directly our heart. Practicing and cultivating feelings of: love, compassion, kindness, forgiveness are secret emotions and feelings that ease one's heart from pain, hardships, traumas etc… They can enrich your life, health and connection to yourself and a higher universal field. In the Holistic methodology acts of kindness, gratitude, compassion, love, and forgiveness are very important and advance a student's practice. The first 100 years of a human life may be the most difficult to surpass because we know little about ourselves, how to use our inner inventory to survive, and hold so much pain, trauma, and loss in our hearts. It is vital to remove negative emotions and practice positive emotions. Emotions can truly change one's world and the entire world. The quicker one practices positive emotions and the Holistic methodology, one can reverse aging, prolong life, and become happier and more youthful. Our bodies are made to last 400 - 900 years, however; today our life spans are significantly shortened because we are not using our mind, heart, and body correctly. Genesis 5, the Book of the Generations of Adam, lists that Adam lived to 930 years old, Seth lived to 912 years, and Enoch to 905 years old. Their long-life span was believed to have existed in order to increase Earth's population, gain knowledge, and the climate was more like a green house effect. There were mild climates that offered more protection from radiation before the flood occurred. After the flood, life spans decreased enormously. Our cells constantly rebuild and re-create themselves.

The Holistic methodology fast forwards some of the knowledge to improve, continue and heal ourselves in our lives. The healing and change begins when we accept our connection with the divine and all things, and feel and love our earth and everything in it. We must love without judgement, ego, and attachment and understand how the universe works. Be grateful, and count your blessings daily.

In conclusion, humans are made to love, and the more you can re-train your heart to love everything in and outside of you then you are more prone to live a joyous human life. To be able to speak directly to the divine, one must practice compassion, kindness, love, feeling and open their hearts. One must let go of the pre-conditioned mind, and allow the heart and feelings to lead our lives. This is what the divine asks, and the right way to go. We do not need to take the hard way in life, and beat ourselves up with judgment and egoism, hatred, and fear. The solution is very simple. Open your heart, be kind, forgiving, loving, compassionate, grateful and speak from your heart to the universal field. You can be a powerful creator of your reality when you unleash your heart with genuine emotion.

Your Subconscious

Our subconscious is the most powerful extended part of our conscious mind. It controls our: breathing, digesting, and forming memories in our inner world. The subconscious is power without direction, and does what it is directed to do. Your life today is what it is because of what your subconscious was fed during your childhood.

To clearly visualize the subconscious, imagine the top of the mountain. The top of the mountain is your 5% conscious mind, and 95% rest of the mountain is your subconscious mind. Everything that we absorb in our conscious mind is sent to our subconscious mind. The subconscious mind retrieves, stores all data, including our: experiences and beliefs.

"Your subconscious makes your beliefs come true. I believe and therefore I am."

-Julie Rammal

If we look at children, from birth to around 2 years of age, a child's brain waves are usually delta waves. Delta waves are low frequency, and this is why babies usually can not stay awake for long. Adults incur delta waves during sleep. From ages 2-6, children live in the zeta wave of imagination or abstract. They live directly from their subconscious mind, and barely filter or judge anything. Their EEG numbers begin to slightly increase as they get older, and everything that is said to them forms their beliefs. They absorb information into their subconscious minds through their sensory systems. From around 6- 8 years of age, their brain waves change to be more alpha waves, and they use their analytical mind to make conclusions of the outer world. During this age, children still live in the pretend and in the real world. Role playing, pretending, and imagination are still important.

From approximately 8- 12 years old, the brain activity rises into higher frequencies as the conscious mind expands. At the age of 12, the gate between a child's subconscious and conscious mind usually closes. As a result, children live in a beta wave where logic, reasoning, and alertness are dominant. As the child grows, they begin to live in low range beta to high range waves until adulthood. Therefore, the lives we live as adults, are exactly what was absorbed to us until approximately 7 years of age. As one grows to adulthood and lives in the awakened state, they begin to experience: stress, anxiety, and other mental issues such as: depression, ADHD, and poor reasoning. The solution for all mental issues is to understand the development of our subconscious and conscious mind, and to calm it through taking it back to a delta state through meditation. In this state, we can re program our subconscious, repeat our new beliefs, and transform ourselves.

Before we learn how our subconscious mind works, allow us to explore the questioning stages that children enter so we can learn how to better communicate with our subconscious.

Children ask questions to gather information of their external world. They can ask questions, through gazing, pointing, touching, or curious looks. It is not until a child is 2.5 -3 years old, that they can verbally communicate a question. The first question that children usually start expressing is "what is dat or that?" at around 21-24 months. At 25- 28 months, the tonality of questions rise. At 26- 32 months, questions such as "where" start to appear. At 36- 40 months, the "who" questions start to rise. At 27 – 42 months, the "is, do" questions appear. At 42- 49 months children explore the "how, why, when" questions.

Now that we understand the stages of questioning, we can learn the subconscious rules to understand our subconscious mind.

1. It does not know what is real from unreal
2. Time is slow
3. Every thought causes a physical reaction
4. You receive what you expect and visualize
5. It is always watching, listening
6. It is stronger then the conscious
7. Ideas stay until they are challenged
8. More conscious mind is used, the less the subconscious mind is used

As we explored the stages of childhood questions, we can must also use similar questions to talk to the subconscious mind. The subconscious mind understands the same childhood questions of "what, where, how, who, what if" questions.

"The what, where, how, who, what if are golden subconscious question that it recognizes."

-Julie Rammal

For example, we can communicate directly with our subconscious mind when we say, "What areas of my life do I need to change immediately to increase my finances? What can I do to be happy? How can I be healthy? How can I attract more friends? What if everything comes to me just like I imagined it?" The subconscious mind loves visualization, you must imagine and see it like a child would for it to manifest. As Einstein said, "Imagination is more important then knowledge." True manifestation can only come with imagination, emotions, belief, heart. If you do not truly believe, ask, see, feel, then do not expect much change to manifest.

Your Brain

Our brains are holographic, and information that enters our brain is distributed within itself. It is divided into 3 major parts: cerebrum, cerebellum and brainstem. The Cerebrum is the largest part of the brain and consists of the right and left hemispheres. The right hemisphere is responsible for: intuition, creativity, imagination, music, and insight. While the left is for: analytical, numbers, logic, math, science, and reasoning.

The division of our brains can also be seen as divided in super conscious, subconscious, and conscious. In the near future, technology is exploring the idea of brain chips to help humans download information faster. This idea is not recommended. We can download the same and much more information by accessing our inner powers to get the information from the Akashic fields.

Your Gift

Your gift is your talent and what are you here on this planet for. What do you truly love to do? What talents comes so naturally to you? Once you find your gift, you can define targets, goals and a vision to grow and enrich your gift with purpose. Once you have purpose, you gain skills, and discipline to focus to reach and perfect your talents, goals and vision. It is important to live our lives freely and to discover one's inner gifts. The true key to success, happiness, joy, and change is to connect back with your inner gift. Examples of inner gifts are: acting, singing, drawing, swimming, cooking, basketball, football, building, driving, sports, public relations, writing and so forth. To truly change our direction in our maze, we must connect back to our inner voice of what we are meant to do. Many business owners start from scratch, doing what they love, and as they follow their inner passion their business expands. You must put your heart, and emotion in your gift, and it will thrive larger than you can imagine. Your true life will begin when you excel in your gift and share that with the world.

Self- Discipline

Once you find your inner talent of gift, it is important to train it with discipline so you fine tune your skills to the best of your ability. Discipline is self-control, and one of the most important acts to surpass change and to change. It gives one structure, stability, character, and promotes good human behaviour. Steve Pavila, a self-help author stated that discipline is, "Acceptance, Willpower, Hard Work, Industry, and Persistence." To gain discipline, we must know our weaknesses, remove temptations, build self-discipline with routine sleeping, exercise, and eating patterns, replace old with new positive habits, train your will power, and forgive yourself and move forward. The Holistic methodology teaches discipline through learning and practicing how to control the subconscious, mind, body, thoughts, emotions and movement. It teaches you internal self-communication and discipline while training you to the best of your ability.

Who Are You?

Once we possess discipline it is important to dig deep down to who you are. In your maze, many things and people may distract or try to change you. It is very important to build a solid identity of who you are with boundaries. When we ask our self, or friends and family, "Who are you?" We often get very different responses for something that may sound so simple. "Who are you?" is a difficult question to answer because most of us are not connected to who we really are. Society, culture, environment may have changed who we are taking away our ability to be present, live, play, enjoy life carefree. We should remove those outer shells, and be able to freely know and answer "Who am I?" Friedrich Wilhelm Nietzsche was a famous German philosopher who truly challenged the universal truth. He said, "All psychology so far has got hung up on moral prejudices and fears, it has not dared to descend to the depth." His response to what the human was, is that "It is a thing dark and veiled; and if the hare has seven skins, the human can slough off seventy times seven and still not be able to say, 'Now that is what you really are, that is no longer outer shell." (Untimely Meditations III). Most people are afraid to descend to their complex inner depth, because it requires effort, and may take one to the unknown place. Most are afraid to exit their comfort zone, and end of living in a superficial layer of their psyche. Nietzsche believed that anyone who entered their inner depth would enter a maze with many dangers that life would bring with it. One could "Lose his way, become solitary, and is torn to pieces by some cave-minotaur of conscience." (Beyond Good and Evil). In other words, if one did not know how to step in and outside of themselves, they could become insane. There are many people who have entered their inner depth, and successfully succeeded such as: Johann Wolfgang von Goethe. Goethe was born in 1749 and created and disciplined himself to wholeness. Despite his inner adventure, he was also a German writer, poet, novelist and worked as an actor, scientist, geologist, botanist, and philosopher. In conclusion, practicing: mastery, control, and discipline must be done when diving within, or you can get lost with no return.

On further note, Nietzsche believed that the surviving nature of each person creates definite limits of who they can become. "The past of every form and way of life, of cultures that formerly lay right next to or on top of each other, now flows into us 'modern souls' our drives now run back everywhere; we ourselves are kind of chaos," as written in the Beyond Good and Evil book. He believed to know our self, we must look and learn from history, as history runs within us. No matter how modern, or sophisticated one may appear, the past history continues to live in their culture and physce and it should be honoured. Each person is an evolved version of history, and if one doesn't understand this, they can also get lost. It is important to build strong foundations and roots of who you are, where you are from, in order to understand your present and future. Possessing a consciousness of our past, having faith in ancient history is something we should have to mentally, physically, and spiritually ignite ourselves. Our current and future generations are facing restlessness in the modern world. This will only continue to grow if we can not properly evolve to the new era. Nitzsche said, "The sense of well-being of a tree for its roots, the happiness to know oneself in a manner not entirely arbitrary and accidental, but as someone who has grown out of a past, as an heir, flower, and fruit." Today, we are still prehistoric humans that have instincts and drives. Our physce still reaches back to primitive drives. He stated, "I have discovered for myself that ancient humanity animality, indeed the entire primal age and past of all sentient being continues in me to love, hate, and to infer." It is important to channel psyche and energy to vitalize life. He said that the modern human relies only on their consciousness, "the weakest and most fallible organ" (On the Genealogy of Morality). He also said that the modern individual "Has lost and destroyed his instinct, and can no longer trust the 'divine animal' and let go the reins when his understanding falters and his way leads through deserts." (Untimely Meditations II). As a result, we live in an inner chaotic world, because the present, pre-historic, and animal instincts contributes to gross contrary impulses within us. As Nitzsche believed, our minds look like a collection of interwoven psychological units, inner rivalry, and conflicting inner personalities. He said, "The most general picture of our essences is an association of drives, with constant rivalry and particular alliances with each other.". When we understand where we are today, and who we are, we can start to feel whole, and pursue our goals, or aims. As Heraclitus of Ephesus, a pre-Socratic Ionian Greek philosopher (born in 535 BC) said, "The world was in harmony with reason, and that everything flows. If you went in search for it, you would not find the boundaries in the soul (psyche), though you travelled every road, so deep is its measures (logos)." Discovering, controlling, and finding yourself is very important to live a life with purpose.

Thought

Our thoughts have vibration, and disciplining our thoughts can excel or stop our entire transformation. Positive thoughts will help you move forward to pursue your aims, while negative thoughts can keep you stagnant, and move you backwards. Most of us struggle with sowing the right thoughts, and as a result experience the wrong life. Our thoughts are our life, and time, mental peace are important in cultivating your thoughts. Your thoughts will only reap when they are clear and direct, and can become more powerful when they are tied to positive feeling through your heart. Every feeling and thought should make your heart pound. We find clear, direct thoughts when we practice meditation and calm our brain frequencies. Be wary of the negative thoughts that always seem to creep in every time. Every negative thought is tied to negative emotions, negative world, and will drag you down. Upgrade your thought system by using positive words such as, "Amazing, beautiful, shining, absolutely, surely, wow, outstanding…" and love everything around you. Create that simple curious childlike mind where everything is amazing. If you get negative thoughts, your feelings and emotional states may change. Negative emotions will always try to stop one from pursuing oneself, and this is why in the Holistic methodology one is taught to always persist, believe in yourself, and never give up. When we find our inner courage and open our black boxes, one will live better than those who live in their fears. As Ralph Waldo Emerson said "Do the thing you fear and the death of fear is certain." When we realize how delicate life is, we take action. Steve Jobs explicated this and said, "Remembering that I'll be dead soon is the most important tool I've ever encountered to help me make the big choices in life. Because almost everything- all external expectations, all pride, all fear of embarrassment of failure- these things just fall away in the face of death, leaving only what is truly important. Remembering that you are going to die is the best way I know to avoid the trap of thinking you have something to lose. You are already naked. There is no reason not to follow our heart." It is very important to constantly evolve, transform, find and develop yourself. As life and everything around us evolves, we must too. When we get stuck, we go against the flow of life. We will start to have physical, emotional, physic, breakdowns, or face serious issues and feelings of guilt, depression, anxiety etc… Keep your thoughts positive, empowering, and fulfilling.

The Psychology Of Transformation

The psychology of transformation also relies on releasing the past, being active, changing your mental state, and perform things as if you are teaching them with emotion and passion. Emotion gives life, and feeling, and to the body, mind and spirit, emotion with information fills up your long-term memory.

To change it is very important to learn and do things with a positive feeling. To re-connect with your inner child qualities and act with curiosity and astonishment. Flipping our mental state to being like a child will also help in transformation. One must "feel the thing (they) ought to be beating beneath the thing (they) are" and push themselves to change as Phillips Brooks, an American Episcopal clergyman and author stated. If we ignore these feelings, then we will remain the same. Once you feel, and accept, change may rise. Carl Jung, a Swiss psychiatrist and psychoanalyst, said, "We cannot change anything unless we accept it." In whatever we do in life, it is important that we observe our feelings and emotions. If we feel: depressed, anxious, stressed, afraid, guilty, negative, we might not be approaching life adequately. As these feelings are the neurotic symptoms that you are not living in harmony within and outside of yourself and you should change. Even though most people may come across these feelings numerous times, it is important to not flee from these emotions but to change their behaviours to develop a different feeling. Many people distract themselves, or take substances as they flee from these emotions. Carl Jung stated, "We may think there is a safe road. But that would be the road of death. Then nothing happens any longer- at any rate, not the right things. Anyone who takes the safe road is as good as dead." Once we accept that change is needed, we then must decide which change is required. Abraham Maslow, an American psychologist studied those who excelled in life. He said that successful people are "motivated by trends to self-actualization," and possess "an ongoing actualization of potentials, capacities and talents, as fulfilment of (a) mission, as a fuller knowledge of, and acceptance of, the person's own intrinsic nature, (and) as an unceasing trend toward unity." It is very important to fulfill your talents and potentials, or you will never be truly happy. Remember to change may not be easy. It is not easy to unsolidify our: thoughts, actions, experiences, beliefs, and habits. However; where there is a will there is a way. As Ralph Waldo Emerson stated to transform you must, "Sow a thought and you reap an action; sow an act and you reap a habit; sow a habit and you reap a character; sow a character and you reap a destiny."

In conclusion, the Holistic methodologies emphasizes understanding principles that govern ourselves and our world such as the: code of the universe, fractals, energy, patterns, maya, vibration, heart, belief, thoughts, mind, subconscious, our gifts or talents, and self-discipline. Every part of us has its own inner code and life force that we must honor, re-connect with, and work with accordingly to possess internal harmony within and outside of ourselves.

Chapter 5:

What is the Holistic Movement

The Holistic Movement is the awakening, education, training, discipline, and love of the entire body, mind and soul that honours and integrates ancestral philosophies to help the human specie adapt and transition into the new era as a human being.

From previous chapters, we have learnt that the human specie is evolving to a new specie that is wired outward rather than inward. This new wiring of artificial intelligence will grow drastically within us over time and cause the human specie to lose: feeling, emotion, awareness, cognitive skills, intuition, natural human abilities, natural movement, connection, and perhaps one's entire self. We must re-connect to ourselves and the universe to know who we are and elevate our body, mind, and soul with the universe. When our connection to ourselves, body, mind and soul are uplifted one will not experience disruptions in body, mind, emotions and soul. The Holistic methodology is our training of self-mastery, education, and discipline to: awaken, rewire, re-connect our body, mind and soul.

"The Holistic methodology honors our ancestral knowledge, practices, and strives to revive the dying human race through the power of re-connecting, training, and disciplining the body, mind, and soul."

-Julie Rammal

Root Cause of Dis-connection

The root cause of our dis-connection has mainly risen from our separation from nature, lack of inner awareness, consciousness, and belief that our conscious minds know better. Our bodies, mind, and soul must be supported and guided for this change in evolution. We must remember that whatever we do to ourselves and earth will return back to us. We must awaken ourselves to preserve nature and our human race. We possess immense powers to change and learn from our ancestors, nature, history, and inner self. Our earth needs us to take care and love everything within it, including ourselves. We should continue to evolve with self-mastery and conscious awareness, and remain connected to our earth and universe. If you do not have this connection, we can easily enter life's vacuum of distraction and larger control systems. The majority of us have allowed our: environments, lifestyles, trends, gadgets to enter our: body, mind, and soul unconsciously. We must use our senses to spot distractions that can dis-balance our entire self and system. We must awaken and nurture our body, mind and soul and give positive life and love to each part of ourselves. The Holistic methodology helps create a life that is for us, rather than against us. The symptoms of human dis-connection are: illness, disease, mental, emotional, physical and spiritual unbalances that affect the human specie on all levels. This can only be reversed and stopped when we choose to re-connect within, and self-master ourselves with curiosity, while plugging our body, mind and soul harmoniously back to the universe with the aid of the Holistic methodology.

> *"The Holistic Movement is our body and mind medicine to survive*
> *in and outside of ourselves today and in the future."*
> -Julie Rammal

Future of Our Health

The future of our health is in serious risk, as more diseases and chronic illnesses, pandemics will rise in: cardiovascular, immunity, respiratory, digestive issues and more. Our entire system is subject to collapse if we do not inter-connect within ourselves to establish our own healing systems, energy, life force, and power.

According to Yale School Of Forestry and Environmental Studies, the climate change may bring mosquitos that will wipe out half of the human population by 2050!

In 2020 the coronavirus pandemic shocked the world with its rapid global spread that shut down airports, business, schools and more. Such unfortunate pandemics will continue to rise along with illnesses, diseases and more because the world is changing, and we are not abiding to the universal laws of life, humanity, and the universe. We are evolving away from ourselves and our world. We must flow with nature, and never go against it because the earth does not need us, however; we need it. We must practice observing, hearing, and listening to mother nature and the universe. We must re-connect as one human race to protect our environment, species, ourselves, future generations, and everything within it.

The Holistic methodology focuses on building a strong internal system that is less dependent on the external in order to survive, connect, heal and overcome illness, challenges, and sicknesses. New minor practices such as Inedia may be our sole future conception of survival along with the Holistic methodology. Inedia is a Hindu based practice and belief that people can live off of the prana, or life force, and do not need to eat or drink. This similar life force is also used in the Holistic methodology for healing, living, and existing. It is important that we begin to turn inwards to understand and re-connect within ourselves and to honour earth, the universe and ancestral knowledge. The time is now.

The Holistic methodology teaches us how to open and unblock our inner powers to feel naturally: happy, energized, youthful, healthy and to live in connection the universal laws of existence.

Holistic Methodology Formula

The success of the Holistic methodology follows a simple recipe for re-creating, tuning, and connecting the body, mind and soul. Its' formula can be thought of as peeling the pre conditioned layers that have blocked and unbalanced our mind, body, and soul and to re-connect them to a higher source of energy.

The Holistic Movement recipe follows the UCEE equation for body, mind, and soul.

UCEE Holistic Movement Equation For Body, Mind And Soul

UCEE Stands for:

UNBLOCK

CONNECT

EMPOWER

EXPAND

With the UCEE formula, the body, mind and soul can return to its' natural state of being.

Unblock = To unblock major body, energy, mind and spiritual blockages that stop or slow down our systems function, transformation process to connect, empower, and expand.

Connect = To connect inward to all of our body, mind, spiritual systems and the universe.

Empower = To train the body, mind and soul with mastery, positivity, and self-discipline.

Expand = To grow and improve body, mind, soul with Holistic Movement and ancient philosophies. To create and build: awareness, movement, knowledge, concentration, discipline, energy, vibration, and overall self-connection within oneself and the universe.

The physical, mental, spiritual training, education and discipline are designed to harmonize body, mind, and soul to raise self and universal connection.

Holistic Body Movement

The ideal Holistic body may return at any age to looking, feeling, and similarly being like one's younger version of themselves.

In the Holistic movement training, the body is trained as one system, or whole, and the major muscles of abdominal, back, legs, spine, frontal and back of arms are always trained in each physical training session with discipline, flow, coordination, breath, focus, and awareness. Exercises can be sequenced, or spot specific for certain muscle groups such as: triceps, back, legs and so forth. The Holistic body appearance is natural, energized, alive and vibrant, flexible, possess natural balanced muscular structure, upright posture, youthful, is unblocked, and easy to move in and outside of itself. The physical training is harmonious, and follows the language that the body understands to: lose weight, detox, feel energized, healthier, happier, and more youthful.

"The Holistic methodology gives life to our bodies, mind and soul."

-Julie Rammal

Session Format

Every class or session begins with the re-connection exercise that focuses on bringing awareness to re-connecting body, mind, soul and breath together. Once this exercise is performed, a 15-minute classic Holistic full body warm up is conducted for all muscles and joints. The warm up is required for class entry, because in the Holistic methodology and belief, if a body is trained while it is physically blocked then we will only be creating more blockages and resistance. Therefore, we must first unblock and prepare the system, stretch, then naturally strengthen, and end the session or class with: flexibility, mental, breathwork conditioning, and universal connection. Secondly, the warm up exercises are designed to build awareness in major muscle groups, and joints in order to give life and feeling to each body part, and reduce the risk of injury.

Re-Connection Exercise
Performed at the start of the session reminds us to breath,
and connect body, mind, spirit.

Each session or class ends with the 3 Arm circle exercise, representing re-connection of: body, mind and soul to the universal fields of energy.

Three Arm circle exercise, representing: body, mind and soul connection to the universe field of energy conducted at close of every class or session.

Holistic Movement Divisions

The Holistic Movement is divided into 5 divisions including education, training and discipline in: body, mind, soul, healing, and living. All 5 divisions are important to fulfil, practice and engage in if one wants to have a Holistic self and life.

One can choose their level, education, and goals, however; to fully master oneself one must complete all training and education levels. Those who wish to further pursue their training must book private consultations, and engage in additional workshops.

The Holistic Movement divisions are divided as seen:

BODY

Physical training includes: re-connection to internal and external bodily systems such as: heart, breath, muscles, joints, and physical black box opening. Methods of: balance, control, endurance, stillness, power, strength, and awareness are exercised through natural primal and body movement. Concepts of: awareness, breath, repetition, consistency, discipline, flexibility, posture are high emphasized.

MIND

Mental training includes: mental conditioning through: silencing mind, repetition, consistency, discipline, black box opening, unblocking and rewiring: emotions, subconscious mind, thoughts, beliefs, vision.

SOUL

Spiritual training includes: Holistic meditation, black box opening, breathwork, gratitude, compassion, energy, soul nurturing, sounds, colors, self-vibration and frequency. Holistic meditations can be conducted with various focal points such as: healing, abundance, purpose, prosperity, love and so forth.

HEALING

Healing training includes: inner system awareness and inner communication, black box opening, breathwork, energy work, sounds, crystals, balancing Ayurvedic Dosha's, food guidelines, release of oppressed emotion stored in system.

LIVING

Holistic living training focuses on rebuilding a Holistic: inner home, environment, friends, family, energy field, and engaging in natural eating, sleeping, and movement routines that honour the circadian rhythms.

Within the Holistic methodology, one can choose to focus on one or more systems to evolve and grow into depending where the need is, and where one is in their lives. All classes and sessions are conducted as beginner, intermediate and advanced levels.

The beginner student learns the basics of each division, and then can pursue one or all divisions to improved their knowledge to intermediate and advanced levels.

The most advanced student is perceived as living the Holistic methodology and all Holistic divisions while being Holistic in body, mind and soul. They are free from major and minor physical, mental and spiritual blockages. They have extraordinary internal and external awareness, can perform body scan, aura, energy scans, open and reawaken subconscious mind or conscious instantly. They are able to perform all of the Holistic body exercises and warm up routines alone, self-heal, meditate, use different breathing techniques, and have a higher connection to self and the universe. They can control major internal systems, open 3rd eye, alter fields of energy, use chi or energy, color, sound, perform eye projection, manifest their desires through: thought, belief, subconscious connection, and can easily alter and train from mental, physical and spiritual state. They are fully inter- connected, and have a high vibration of existence with a positive attitude. They abide and follow the Holistic methodology practices, values and execute and engage in all philosophies naturally without added effort in their life. It can take up to 10-15 years to reach this level of advanced self-mastery.

"Your body is an empire, and when you are connected to you, you can achieve miracles."

-Julie Rammal

Holistic Movement Training Divisions

1. Body & Physical Training
2. Mind Training
3. Healing
4. Living
5. Education

While further engaging in the Holistic methodology, students learn various important concepts that the methodology addresses such as the: Life Maze, Beaded Necklace (Chapter 2), Black Box, and Eye and Field projection. Other concepts are kept confidential and presented when a student has demonstrated their abilities and performance on all Holistic methodology levels and practice.

Black Box

The **Black Box** are blocked or distorted energy, frequency, vibration and areas in our body, mind, heart, lungs, soul, and subconscious that make us: ill, negative, depressed, anxious, lazy, weak, un-balanced, afraid, sick, confused, lack purpose and vision, low confidence, stressed, inability to concentrate, poor sensory skills, lack of eye contact, lack of creativity, insomnia, eating disorders, lack of strength on all systems, lack of motivation, lack of goals and vision, unhappiness, pain etc…

They are similar to chakras, however; chakras are focal points in the subtle body, denominated in tantra and esoteric traditions. Black Boxes are perceived to be in the physical, energetic, and mental layers of the body and are opened through Holistic practices that include: awareness, energy trigger therapy, repetition, and removing and re-training blocked layers that are surmounted in the Black Box areas. These layers are worked on in the Holistic methodology to fine tune and unblock blocked energy, improve and circulate energy, frequency, energy, vibration, and emotions in heart, mind and body.

According to Vedantic philosophy, we have 3 bodies that include our physical, subtle, and casual bodies that cover our 5 koshas or sheath layers. If we think of ourself as an onion, in our life various events, thoughts, experiences get stored and collected in various layers. The outermost layer of our onion is our physical body. The second layer is our energetic body. The third layer is our mental layer. The fourth layer is our wisdom layer. The fifth layer is our bliss layer, and the deepest layer is our true spiritual self. Through meditation, practice, holistic meditations and consultations, and awareness one can access and alter various blockages in several layers.

Our Black Boxes rapidly fill up during our childhood years as: friends, family, environment, trends, music, media, food, pollution, negativity, toxicity quickly get absorbed in certain parts and layers that later affect us. Trauma can severely affect these locations. Our Black Boxes are clear when we are born, and then can evolve to become semi or fully blocked. The Holistic methodology perceives them as areas in our system that slow down or stop us from progress or transformation in life, body, mind, soul and make us: lack inner confidence or power, unhappy, lack energy, and can age and lead one to an unhealthy road path.

If we do not clean up our own Black Boxes, we end up living a life of what's stored in our system. Do you remember your teacher, or parents telling you "You don't know how to do that, or you can't do that!" Over time if that message is absorbed repetitively into your subconscious box, soon or later one will realize that they may lose confidence, and feel they really can't do something. As a result, one might even turn introvert, or become depressed. Of course, there are rules in life, you can't do everything otherwise we will end up living and being in a chaotic society. Another example may rise from breathing toxic and polluted air overtime, or smoking and inhaling pollutants, your lungs develop Black Boxes that can affect your body, mind and spirit. It can be the root cause of why you are not spiritually connected to a higher source of power. Our youthful years, circle of friends and social life can also create mental Black Boxes. Were you surrounded by positive, inspirational leaders, or by negative experiences, and things? Who and what did you learn from and hang out with while you were growing up? Your mental box stores all of your education, experiences, cognitive and survival skills, which can affect your subconscious, body, heart, soul, and lung box!

In the Holistic mind sessions, we work on clearing and re-patterning these blockages and re-connect and align ourselves to a higher universal field to experience health, abundance, manifestations, new behavior or thought patterns and more. It is important, to remember to re-enter your boxes, and unblock, connect, empower, expand (UCEE) every Black Box if you truly want to change.

Black Box Sites

Black Boxes are located mainly in our: **body, mind, subconscious, soul, heart, lungs** and usually come from: people, environment, experiences, culture, negativity, toxicity, trauma, poor posture, poor or contaminated nutrition, bad experiences, and repetitive brainwashing or subconscious/ subliminal messages.

System's Black boxes: subconscious, mind, body, soul, heart, lungs

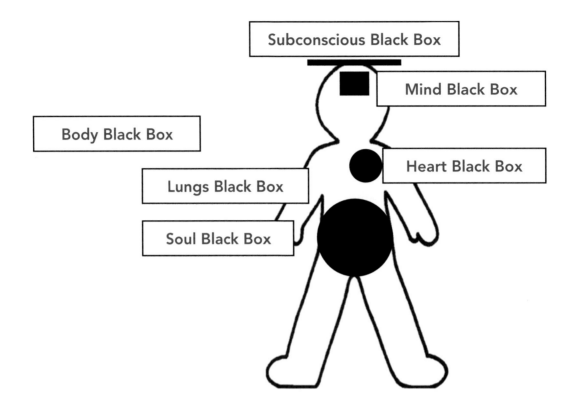

When our Black Boxes are clear, we will experience improved: thought, energy, mental clarity, confidence, creativity, vision, inner and external power, happiness, and youthfulness. We can easily communicate with our subconscious and the universe, and are forgiving, loving, flexible, pain free, and have limited fear. However; very few of us are aware of these Black Boxes, simply because most of us live a routine life in our comfort zone, and lack awareness of ourselves. When our Black Boxes are closed, we can not see the light in life, and continue to live in the dark while we think we are living. Our body may have little or no feeling, and is blocked with low energy and vibration. When our Black Boxes are clear we can see beyond, have purpose, mission, clarity, open heart, mind, spirit, and can feel joy, happiness, success, and love.

Black Box Symptoms

The most common symptoms of locked or semi locked Black Boxes are: lack of confidence or feeling of wholeness and purpose, lack of focus, depression, overall negative sense of feeling, lack of inner power and strength, over or under activity, shy, insomnia, irregular eating patterns, eating disorders, improper breathing cycles, emotional instability, lack of vision, unstable mind, sadness, depression and so forth.

Unblocking Black Box

The first step to unblock your Black Box is to be aware of it and the symptoms, then to make a decision to change one or all Black Box's state. With a strong mind set, awareness, training, discipline, repetition, consistency, and engaging in the Holistic therapies and methodologies the Black Boxes will start to open and change their states. For example, running is a natural activity. If one feels they do not like to run, their Black Boxes need to be opened. Once they are opened, they can again become a wonderful runner. During the Black Box opening practices, concepts such as: awareness, vision, understanding, commitment, and self-work and inner motivation are improvised. The act of decision and acknowledgement, as we learnt in chapter 1 is the first step to create space for change to follow. The Holistic methodology can increase the rate of change by practicing skills such as: re-connection, self-reflection, ancient methodologies for healing, self-detoxification and cleansing, de-attachment, and to remove mental, body, and spiritual blockages. One must silence internal and external interferences in order to rebuild, align, and re-gain: power, strength, vision, awareness, self-communication, and success. If the Black Boxes are left untrained and reopened one will not be able to transform or evolve in the long run.

The second step is to stay away from the root blockages of the Black Boxes. For example, if someone has a major lung Black Box, a Holistic movement trainer or practitioner will help find the root cause for this blockage. Once the root cause is addressed, they will advise how to open, empower, protect and train the lung Black Box following the holistic formula. Another example is if someone has irregular breath or short breath cycles, the chances of their lung boxes being affected may be very high. Their lung box may be filled with negative emotions, and blockages that are not allowing them to move forward. The holistic methodology can re-open this box, and holistic movement trainers and practitioners will be able to do so using the holistic formula and methodology.

Once your Black Boxes are re-opened it is very important to understand your place and connection in the universe so you do not fall into life's vacuums, distractions and traps and refill your Black Boxes again. The world is filled with environmental vacuums that de-balance and vacuum our: body, mind, heart, spirit, subconscious, emotions and has the power to overtake a complete human specie. We should not be the product of our culture, environment, society, media, education system and so forth. The real you is the you that was born free, before anything was absorbed into your body, mind, subconscious, and spirit. We should often re-open and fine tune our Black Boxes to progress.

The common symptoms of opened Black Boxes is feeling happy, energized, youthful, and with a clear vision of where one is heading to. The best example of the body reacting and clearing their mental, emotional, and body systems are children. Children normally have tantrums when they are 12 to 18 months old, 2-3 years old, and normally after four years of age they start to decrease. Those tantrums are a beautiful way to clear the body and mind, and express that something is wrong without verbal communication. Once we have mastered our language system, our inner and external communications begin to alter our emotional release, thoughts, beliefs etc... Each individual must work within themselves, re-connect, clear, and reflect on their stance of who they are, and where they are heading to.

To conclude, Black Boxes can cause: self-toxicity, bad habits, and blockages in: body, mind, heart, lungs, subconscious, and soul leaving one to feel: artificial pain, illness, discomfort, lack of vitality, brain fogginess, lack confidence, power, old, and may be mentally, physically, emotionally unbalanced. Our Black Boxes must be opened, protected, and re-programmed to find our true inner and external powers. When the Black Boxes are opened one will feel: confident, motivation, strength, joy, purpose, internal balance, and some may even experience superhuman powers.

Superhuman Powers

In the Holistic methodology, we exercise superhuman powers in advanced training and education. We enhance human qualities, and abilities to improve: intuition, 3rd eye opening, eye projection, projection of energy force fields, improve speed, healing, awareness, senses, telepathic communications, perceiving world from subconscious to conscious and vice versa. Very few people continue to reach this level because it takes many years to excel to. Often private sessions are given to enhance these abilities in students.

In the future, superhuman abilities will be enhanced by genetic modification, cyber implants, or superhuman artificial intelligence. This can all be achieved naturally through the Holistic methodology, with focused: mental conditioning, body training, and knowing oneself.

To gain superhuman powers one must master each training level and practices, and live the Holistic methodology with discipline, awareness, consistency, and remove Black Boxes. Once we train, balance, connect in: body, mind and spirit we will thrive in the direction we pursue to take.

In summary, the Holistic movement was developed to honor the human specie, and re-teach each human to know and master themselves to continue into the next era by engaging ancestral knowledge and philosophies to remain human. The Holistic methodologies are offered in 5 divisions including: education, training mind, body, spirit, healing, and living.

Holistic Methodology Concepts

During the course of one's study, training and journey, major concepts are mastered by each student. The major beginner and intermediate concepts include:

Human Anatomy
Understanding of ancient philosophies and methods
Understanding of universe and our inner systems

Understanding of Holistic methodology, divisions, and practices
Understanding, control, and body awareness
Understanding, control, and mental awareness
Understanding, accessing, and spiritual awareness
Understanding Of Subconscious
Communication with Subconscious
Control of subconscious system
Understanding Of Chakra System
Understanding of Self reflexology points
Understanding Of Black Boxes
Understanding Of Meridian Lines
Understanding Chi and energy
Creating and projecting field of energy
Execution of Eye Projection
Training Sensory systems
Learning and Training Breath
Mastering repetition, consistency and discipline
Learning how to shift from conscious to higher states of awareness and vibration
Mastering of body through holistic warm up, movements and exercises
Equal training and development for: balance, endurance, awareness, control, speed, flexibility, breath, strength, and power
Mastery of moving air to certain system parts such as mind, body.
Mastery of moving energy within and outside of body
Mastery and awareness of nerve movement
Mastery of fluid movement
Mastery of sound, colour, symbols
Mastering outdoor training in all weather conditions
Mastery of self healing techniques
Intuitive and physic powers
Holistic conscious living
Emotional control
Holistic meditation
Holistic self care, detoxification, and cleansing
*Advanced: super human powers

Gaining access to the Holistic Movement

The Holistic movement was originally called JSport because of its primary focus on luxury Holistic Body Training services that were used by celebrities, high profile clients, and VIP's. The Holistic practice went public upon the launch of the world's first Holistic DVD: In Light Of Change in 2016. In 2019 JSport was renamed Holistic Movement, and now offers: consultations, workshops, conferences, retreats, private sessions, teacher trainer study, and group class format online and live. Its' mission is to share the power of the Holistic Movement to create happy, healthy, energized, and youthful humans that are connected in body, mind and soul to themselves and the universe.

Educational workshops and conferences can be seen on facebook page, https://www.facebook.com/byJulieRammal and Instagram: holisticmovement.co

The first world's Holistic DVD: In Light of Change is a two week program to get firmer, slimmer and younger with the Holistic methodology. It is available worldwide in DVD, Mobile APP, and digital form on www.holisticmovement.co. It includes the first Holistic sequence and exercise system to: unblock, strengthen and train the body and mind, open chakras and energy, improve power, focus, posture, breath while benefiting from toning, weight loss, detoxification, increased energy, and youthfulness.

DVD: In Light Of Change, The World's 1st Holistic DVD

The world's first Holistic Youtube channel By: Julie Rammal, is also available, and offers new complimentary training videos for body, mind and soul development. To access and subscribe, follow the link hereunder or search Holistic Movement By: Julie Rammal

https://www.youtube.com/channel/UCRzm_sROjlngtAWY1Jjolyw

Holistic Movement By: Julie Rammal YouTube Channel

To become a Holistic Movement teacher or Holistic mind consultant, and practice and implement the Holistic methodologies, one must apply to be a Holistic movement trainer or consultant or both. Each course includes: manuals, educational tools, exams, certificate, and must demonstrate their knowledge through live and pre-recorded video's.

The Holistic Movement teacher can apply for beginner, intermediate or advanced teacher levels or all three comprehensive levels. The Holistic Movement trainer must study materials provided to them, attend workshops, pass exams, and demonstrate various concepts in the Holistic methodology in order to work with clients. All students are encouraged to continuously study, learn and must renew their certification yearly. All Holistic Movement teachers and consultants' names are added to the list of Holistic trainers and consultants on our website and social media.

The Holistic Movement and its methodologies have been presented and used in: embassies, schools, spa and resorts, bank and government sectors, medical industry, alternative medicine sectors, health clubs and studios and more.

Following www.holisticmovement.co is the best way to be up to date with all activities, events, and education.

Holistic Movement at Conferences, Events, Schools, Seminars worldwide available on
https://holisticmovement.co/gallery

In conclusion, the Holistic Movement is a movement to awaken, empower, re-connect the internal and external body, mind, soul to be human. It offers mental, physical, and spiritual conditioning to create: a strong, flexible, fast, controlled, disciplined, energized, balanced, and youthful individual in spirit. It is the future of movement.

"Holistic movement is the language developed for our body and mind to empower us to our visions."
                                    Julie Rammal

Lastly, the Holistic Movement offers Julie Rammal's luxury clothing and jewelry brand to empowers those to spread their inner light to others. 20% of all purchases are donated to the Holistic Movement's mission. To learn more visit http://www.julierammal.com, Instagram: julie.rammal, FB: https://www.facebook.com/julierammal.lb

Chapter 6:

Self Suppression & Junk

We are living in an age where, from our birth, we are bombarded with information that have controlled our behaviour and attitude and self-supress our innate character. We should build an awareness of the junk we carry, our self-suppression and re-create a beautiful and powerful body, mind and soul with positive emotions that empower us.

We were born free, but, at present, the majority of us are not free. We are dressed up in layers of clothing, emotions, thoughts, beliefs, systems, and labels, and have lost the connection and feeling of what freedom is. As adults or teenagers, we can not act like children and yell, have tantrums, throw things, run naked, and truly express ourselves in public. We have been subjected to many rules, laws, trends, cultures, traditions and more that have pre-conditioned us to abide by. Rules and regulations are listed everywhere we go from: supermarkets, gyms, clinics, hospitals, and stores etc…The majority of us no longer know what the power of freedom is. Freedom is the right to speak, act, behave, and be what one wants to be. We must re-awaken our senses, awareness, and re-connect to positive things that empower us. Once we re-awaken ourselves, we are free from self supressed environments and energy, vibration and connection to a higher source of universal power are automatically raised.

In the Holistic methodology, it is important to work and clear what we have absorbed within ourselves and lives at present in order to evolve the way we choose to be and feel free in our circle of training. As long as there is a will there will be a way, and the door to change and enlighten ourselves from self-suppression is always open.

Self- Suppression

It is important to understand the concept of self-suppression in the Holistic Movement, in order to create an awareness and practice the UCEE formula to unblock, connect, expand and empower ourselves.

From the moment we are born, we are physically suppressed, such as with diapers, clothing, pacifiers, artificial milk, and then in our environments with artificial lightening, sounds, creams, medicine, shots, clothing etc…. As we age, we become more suppressed with things that take us away from our root being. We start to clog our body, mind, and soul unknowingly as we engage in trends of what to believe, purchase, see, feel, experience, and consume.

With unconscious age, our body, mind and soul get immensely suppressed that we often look, act, and think like every label, advertisement, music, video, trend or tv show absorbed into our systems and environments. Our homes and environments are filled with so many ads that we forget the original appearance, simplicity, and taste of our foods, homes, furniture, clothing, and ourselves. When we compare current modern homes to homes 200 years ago, we notice that many of our houses are suppressed with labels, subliminal messages, and distractions that reflect our outer world and leak into our subconscious minds. Many of us turn to organic foods, however; we must remember that the only true organic food is the food that comes with taste, natural texture, color, and beauty from mother earth's creation. Over time, the things that our senses absorb become our reality, and we begin to forget the origin of everything including ourselves.

We should never lose the connection to who and what we are. As we age, our suppression increases and we lose the core root of being: happy, energized, motivated, youthful, happy and joyful. We begin to look like what we see, hear, sense, and become an imprint of our environments. This imprint sticks to us, and can only be removed with awareness and will power. As we lose connection to ourselves, many of us may become: materialistic, egoistic, lose values, emotionally unbalanced, criminals, unproductive, unstable and more. We must build an awareness in order to clear, free ourselves and re-create ourselves and surroundings in order to build life transforming changes, habits, and to manifest our deepest desires of change.

To change and alter the suppressed self we should become aware of our self- suppression. We must take control of what enters our senses, and re-align our mind, body, soul and subconscious with our own internal dialogue and with the one of universe. The history of the human senses was made to see nature and greenery, smell fresh air, hear natural sounds, and taste natural foods. Today, the majority of our senses are distant from what they are meant to be absorbing. A human should look, be and feel beautiful, shine, and maintain a balanced and connected body, mind, and soul with the Divine field. We should free ourselves from the artificial layers that have covered our body, mind and soul to feel again happy, aligned, healthy, and energized.

How Suppression & Junk Affects Our Posture With Age

It is vital that we retrack our lives from the time we were born, and eliminate everything that was added and disrupted our: body, mind, soul, subconscious, beliefs, thoughts, heart, emotions and so forth. We must take a stance to regain our gift, and relive our beautiful life again as a human being free from junk and suppression.

In the same context, our breath is one of major fundamental systems to clear and connect ourselves to a higher power. Our breath reveals the life shocks, traumas, and experiences we have absorbed. Some may experience difficultly, pain or fear to inhale deep breaths. The baggage of mind, body, emotions becomes so heavy for our system to carry alongside with our partially or fully clogged black boxes. Our body, mind and soul cannot carry more weight, and this is why we are seeing a society with growing illnesses, diseases, and mental physical and emotional problems. We must regain our breath to strengthen and build a stronger immunity and better health. As such, we must engage in proper balanced breathing techniques to live in harmony with nature, ourselves, and the divine field.

Everyday should be a blessing for us to do something new, life happier, and more connected to ourselves and our world. It should not be just another day of routine and work. Everyday must have joy, love, happiness, curiosity, movement, creativity, and health. We must re-connect to our joys, beauty of life, and ourselves in order to transform positively in the new era. Our life begins where our heart, body, mind, soul, and awareness are re-connected within and outside of ourselves to the universe. Allow us to re-attach to our inner and outer senses of feeling, emotions, sight, sound, taste, feeling, and hearing to build our inner connections with ourselves and environments.

The Holistic methodology frees our suppression by awareness, meditation, movement, dance, pressure points, and blissful thoughts. To free oneself, one should begin with self-awareness, re-awaken, and detox their senses and self. A powerful ancient Ayurvedic morning ritual can be used to clear our senses, impurities, toxins, and to start our morning in gratitude and happiness.

In the Holistic methodology healing sessions, pressure point may be applied to the body to help remove blockages, restore balance, and healing. The signs of suppression release after such sessions include: curiosity, joy, creativity, focus, eye contact, energy, sense of relief, improved posture and movement skills, happiness and more. It is important to release self-suppression, and re-connect back to the universe and nature. When we lose our connection, or presence, we lose vision, intention, motivation, purpose, and become easily distracted with everything around us and our body and mind systems may collapse.

"Nature is the Holistic methodologies' best friend, so let it be yours."
-Julie Rammal

In conclusion, the Holistic methodology teaches us to own ourselves and lives. The body, mind, and soul should have space to grow, transform and evolve naturally rather than become suppressed with fear, negativity, toxicity and external artificial appearances and things that do not truly reflect our genuine selves.

Ayurvedic Morning Ritual

1. Wake up with gratitude.
2. Perform a tongue scraper ritual to clear the respiratory, digestive, and nervous systems with a stainless steel or copper tongue scraper to remove ama (bacteria, plaque, tongue coating).
3. Drink room temperature water in a copper cup. A copper cup helps balance the three dosha's, prevents illnesses, increases Alkaline properties, kills bacteria, and improves nerve transmission.
4. Begin the Holistic Breath, Chapter 9.
5. Perform a Holistic Meditation for 15-20 minutes, Chapter 9 and 15.
6. Perform a dry brushing ritual for body prior to shower to remove impurities, toxins, improve circulation, exfoliate dead skin cells, clear pores, and improve beauty and health.
7. Perform a whole body scrub.
8. Shower and dry yourself.
9. Gently apply olive or almond oil to nourish and balance the dosha's.
10. Empty colon to clean digestive tract in bathroom.
11. Perform Yoga or Holistic movement exercises to improve body appearance and health.

Anti Suppression Shake Exercise

This exercise is targeted to release, restore emotions, and bring overall body blood circulation.

1. From a standing position, begin to shake your body in all directions. Feel your physical blockages, and try to shake them out. Continue to shake your entire body as if you are having a tantrum, and feel lighter in those blocked areas.
2. Perform for 30 seconds or more, and then take a deep re- balancing breath 5-10 times, and repeat the exercise 5 more times.
3. Once you are done, become present in the moment, and thank your body and mind for clearing your blockages.
4. If you are carrying a lot of mental, physical, emotional blockages then you may need to repeat this exercise for a longer period of time, or more frequently.

5. Upon completing the exercise you can enrich your experience by taking a warm salt bath for 20 minutes with Epsom salts, and then rub a warm soothing organic oil onto your body and lie down on your back. Cover yourself with a blanket for 10- 15 minutes and rest.

Examples of nature oils that can be used are: olive, almond, jojoba oil, coconut oil, or shea butter.

Awakening Exercise

1. From standing position, crunch yourself, tightening all your muscles and nerves, re-emphasizing the stored mental and body tension as seen in position 1 image.

2. Inhale deeply, and as you exhale audibly expand your mouth, chest, and arms horizontally as seen in position 2 image.

3. Complete the Awakening exercise by opening and expanding all muscles and body parts into position 3.

4. Repeat 5-10 times with conscious breath.

5. Upon completion, from seated or standing position, take 3-6 deep re-balancing breaths to ground yourself back and allow your muscles and nerves to naturally stabilize themselves.

Awakening exercise for emotional release and awareness

| *Position 1* | *Position 2* | *Position 3* |

Jump Exercise

1. From a standing position, begin to jump for 30 – 60 seconds in the same spot. Build awareness of what organs, muscles or body parts feel energetically heavier or blocked.

2. Rest for a few seconds and repeat 5 times.

3. Upon completion, from standing position, inhale and exhale 3-6 breaths, directing your breath to blocked areas of your body.

Lastly, to get rid of the suppressed self you can engage in: drawing, art, singing, poetry, music, dancing, Holistic Movement exercises, talking, grunting, yelling, writing, and begin to accept and love the new you.

What is the Junk

You were born free, and yes, I repeat "You were born free!" Freedom is the right to think, act, believe, and be who you are without judgement, conditioning, and programming. Freedom is a gift given to us, but unconsciously taken away during our early years.

The majority of us are self-suppressed with junk. By the age of around 30 years old we start to physically, mentally, emotionally look like what we have fed ourselves on all levels. The opportunity to know ourselves is reduced and as a result we may no longer know who we really are, and continue to drift into various funnel systems that toss and turn us in every direction. This funnel or vacuum system tells you that you must have a career, a title, make xyz amount of money, or do this or that.

If you are reading this book, congratulations, you are seeking a new transformation, a wake up call to your new self, and the Holistic methodology is your guide.

The Holistic Movement is a system that empowers you, and teaches you to re-connect from within to listen to your heart, and follow your inner passions, talents, and desires. We must live the life that we program ourselves to live with our own program that is spiritually connected.

A few of us may start the first step of awareness, however; only few will persist to create time and dedication to understand their internal universe. Those who do not dig deep within themselves, may easily fall into external systems to guide them. Change takes patience, persistence, belief, work, and dedication. You are the strongest being when you know yourself, and have a strong internal connection, belief system, and have little suppression and inner junk. You are truly free when your mind and heart are positive, forgiving, loving, kind, and curious to discover everything within and outside of yourself.

Stop for a moment and think to yourself. Do I want to keep carrying all this junk? Is this junk empowering me and making me happy, healthy, energetic, and youthful? Do I want to be a pre-conditioned and pre-programmed person, or do I want to be myself, and follow what I truly desire, feel and what is good for the world? If you truly want to be yourself again, start removing all the junk. Your life will dramatically change as you clear up suppression and junk. If you do not remove the junk, it may be difficult to subsist into the next era as a human being. You may be able to continue to live, but your deepest inner purpose, happiness, health, and emotions may be challenged through rough waters.

In conclusion, the "junk" is everything that was added to your initial body, mind, emotions, and spirit that was not from within yourself. It may be thoughts, words, beliefs, material things, gadgets, artificial pre-programmed exercise programs, body image, social standing, career, style etc. We must uplift our abilities to think, see, hear, feel and connect from within ourselves, and remove the junk that we carry.

In the upcoming decades, it is vital to re-connect in body, mind, soul, to ourselves and to Earth and the universe. As such, we need to abide to the universal laws, and maintain a spiritual connection to survive the upcoming era challenges.

Remove The Junk

To remove the junk, you must first bring awareness of it, and that you have the deepest desire to clear and remove it from all systems. The real work begins with your self-mastery, exploration, clearing, re-programming, and believing in your ability to have full power, control, and strength over your life.

Remove labels that were given to you, titles, age numbers, trends that funnelled you in, artificial beliefs, identity, emotions, and thoughts. Reflect on your early childhood years, and remember major events, environments, people, food, images that altered your behaviour, thoughts, beliefs and so forth. For example, you might have been told numerous times as a child that you will never succeed in sports, or do not talk loud, or eat a lot of meat to be strong, do not run fast because you might hurt yourself, or do not do this and that.

Very few of us grow up with empowering and positive beliefs that strengthen our confidence and enrich our connection to ourselves and the universe. By the age of 7, we are already pre-programmed to move, act, think, and behave the way: society, laws, schools, parents, or caregivers have formed us to be, and in our mid 30's we start falling apart. We are no longer fed values, ethics, but instead are fed a life full of fear, punishment and do not do's.

We must re-create a Holistic mind as we will learn in Chapter 7 that is filled with human values, ethics and respect for everything in our world. The Holistic Movement helps create a society that is acting upon faith, trust, goodwill, positive beliefs, and connection to ourselves and a higher source of power.

Biggest Junk is Fear

The biggest junk in our body, mind and soul is FEAR. Fear decreases our vibration, plays with our memory, perception of reality, and creates anxiety which later leads to other problems in our body and lives.

Fear is an emotion that exists in animals and humans and its purpose is to promote survival. In the human evolution, fear created survival to do the right things and pass their genes to future generations. Charles Darwin stated that fear is an instinctive tightening of muscles as a response to something fearful or fear itself. Fear should only be used for survival, and not implanted in our minds to take away from our joy, health, energy and youthfulness. Fear has its limits to its usage. Fear should not be used to control or focus concentration daily, but only for unusual or emergency situations.

When we have an excess of fear, our mind, body, and lives will be impacted and, consequently, we will lose the ability to think, feel, and explore new territories of life. Ask yourself, how much fear do you have right now? Are you afraid that someone can break into your house? Are you afraid to talk to the public? Are you afraid of yourself? Are you afraid to dress differently? Excess fear will drown your consciousness, and suffocate your mind and body, and slow down your ability to travel to your vision.

Remove un-needed fear and be yourself.

Red light Exercise

Stare at this image for around 1 minute repeating to yourself, subconscious, and mind that "I choose to stop fear, and junk from entering my body, mind and spirit." You can also stare at this image and repeat the opposite statement for the majority of your fears. For example, if you are afraid of snakes, look at the red circle and state "I am not afraid of snakes." Repeat this exercise daily, or anytime you are feeling fear or absorbing junk. Our mind recognizes symbols, and symbols have a powerful affect on the direction we take in our lives.

Fear Removal and Belief

In the red circle write down all your past or present fears in body, mind, spirit. In the white circle write your new empowering beliefs to know where you stand. You can repeat this exercise anytime you feel that you are returning back to feeling the emotion of fear.

White Light Exercise

Observe the white circle, re-write your positive empowering beliefs in the circle. Stare at the circle and your new positive written beliefs for 1 minute, as your system absorbs them.

This exercise can be done anytime when you feel you need to re-empower your belief systems or you are not exercising them.

Red and White Light Meditation

1. Look at the above image, take a deep inhale, and naturally breathe inhale and exhale 5-10 deep breaths.

2. Think about your new positive empowering beliefs and affirmations that are far away from your fears.

3. Focus on your meditation for 1-3 minutes.

4. Once you are done, open your eyes, smile, and look at the white circle for one minute.

5. You can perform this exercise anytime you feel the negative and fearful mind is returning. Repeat until the fear is dissolved, and the new empowering belief is stronger and alive.

Remove Fear Exercise

1. Write down all of your fears and replace them with the statement I am not afraid of …. (list that fear), written 5 times. For example, the fear is: I am afraid of snakes.

   Write five times: I am not afraid of snakes.

2. You can rewrite them, or mentally repeat them as many times until the fear is removed from your system.

Remove My Junk Exercise

As you may recall, we are made of 5 subtle layers referred to as Koshas. They include:

1. Physical Body (food we eat enters here, our dna, skin, cells, tissue, organs)

2. Energy Body (physiological energy between atoms, cells, organ systems)

3. Mental Body (mind, emotions, feelings, likes, dislikes, fears, phobias)

4. Wisdom Body (higher intellect, consciousness)

5. Bliss Body (Feeling peace, freedom, consciousness expands beyond body)

Take time to write down all the junk in each bodily layer that you feel you have, and begin to build awareness of all of it. For example, what junk did you feed your physical body? How is your breath? Is it smooth and calm or erratic (energy body)? How is your stress? Are you fatigued? How is energy? Does your energy feel different in various parts of your body?

Once you build this awareness on each kosha layer, tell yourself that "I have the power to change my physical, energy, mental, wisdom, and bliss body to be happy, energized and youthful." Say it with passion, feeling, and speak from the heart, and begin the Holistic movement exercises, outdoor training, or consult a holistic movement trainer.

Physical Junk Release

To remove the physical junk:

1. Scan your entire body, or work with a Holistic trainer who knows how to read your physical blockages.
2. On a piece of paper mark all your tense blocked bodily areas.

Physical Junk Release Exercise

Box A

Positive emotions

1.

2.

3.

4.

5.

Box B

Negative emotions

1.

2.

3.

4.

5.

3. Write 5 major negative emotions that you feel you have such as: hate, guilt, disgust, sadness, fear, anger etc…in box B, and five major positive emotions that you have such as: love, faith, hope, joy in box. A.

4. Intuitively connect a line from each emotion to each body part that you have labelled. Wonderful.

5. Now you can see where most of your negative and positive junk is stored - the areas you have marked as the areas storing the majority of your negative or positive emotions.

6. To further cleanse yourself, you must work with a Holistic movement trainer or practitioner.

Tantrum Exercise

1. Lie down comfortably on your back with arms at the side of your body and legs spread out 1-2 feet.

2. Take a deep breath, and have a child like tantrum, shaking, yelling, grunting for 1 minute. Repeat step 2 for 1-5 times.

3. When done, restore balance to your body by taking 5-10 deep breaths, and then standing up, and ending with the 3 arm circle exercise (Chapter 5).

4. To perform the 3 arm circle, stand tall, lengthen your arms upwards, and gently circle both of your arms backwards as you breathe in the first circle for your body, second for mind, and third for soul or spirit.

Release Your early childhood mental junk

There are many ways to remove our mental junk, but firstly the success of it depends on a strong conviction and decision. Some of us may have so much determination and belief that just by saying aloud may actually be enough as such:

"I choose to release and remove all my old mental junk. Today is a new day, and my mind is fresh, clear and open to new experiences."

For others, the mind has to be dug into, and certain imprints, programs, pre-conditioning, and junk have to be extracted. This is what many therapists such as NLP, hypnotherapists, and some psychologists help one do. Are you ready to try to rewind your mental tape?

1. Sit in a calm and quiet place

2. Take a deep breath, and rewind your mind back to when you were a child

3. Imagine being in that very moment

4. What kind of messages do you remember hearing, seeing, feeling? Remember your first supermarket experience, school, friends, toys, environment, etc…

5. Think about subconscious advertisements you were always exposed to in supermarkets, certain candy, ice cream brands, and all negative dis-empowering statements that you were given or told

6. Re-connect even deeper to your past childhood memories

7. Take a moment to write down some of the major statements you can recall. For example:

✓ I am not a good runner
✓ I will never be good in math
✓ I am too fat
✓ I have an ugly nose
✓ Etc.

8. When you have written at least 10-20 of them cross them out and write, feel, and audibly say the exact opposite statement that you wrote. Write each opposite statement 3-5 times. For example,
   ✓ I am a great runner
   ✓ I am a great runner
   ✓ I am a great runner
   ✓ I am very good in math
   ✓ I am very good in math
   ✓ I am very good in math

9. When done, close your eyes and visualize to see in detail each new written statement. Imprint this visualization in your mind.

10. You can repeat this exercise for several weeks, until everything is well conditioned and planted.

11. Once you are able to audibly say your new statements with confidence, and assertiveness then you have succeeded.

Erase ALL the junk

Let us begin by clearing our junk even further.

A- Grab a pen and notebook and follow the following exercises. Complete each exercise in as much detail as you can, as if you are re-living the past again.

1. Your Pre-programmed name

2. Your birthday and age

3. Your current profession, studies, professional background

4. Your emotional state (are you happy, depressed, etc…)

5. Your current beliefs (I believe that I must exercise to lose weight, I believe that I must work hard to succeed at work or in business, or to support my family and my community, or to become more prosperous or get richer, etc…)

B- Now, scratch points 1-5. Write, believe, and audibly say with confidence 10 times:

"I delete all of my pre-programmed beliefs, thoughts, and label systems. I have a new belief and thought system. I am clear from all past beliefs, thoughts, and labels. I am worthy of a new life. I am clear."

C- Describe and in detail write the first 7 years of your childhood (include your emotions, thoughts, feelings, toys, schools, teachers, environment, food, medicines and any other details as if you are reliving those past 7 years all over again). Write out all the junk, and do not be afraid to let go.

D- Describe and in detail write your life from 7-15 years including all details of thoughts, emotions, environment, feelings, conflicts etc....

E- Now scratch what you wrote. Write and audibly say with confidence 10 times:

"I delete the first 7-15 years of my childhood life. I affirm that all events, feelings, thoughts, emotions are 100% cleared from my body, and my mind. I am cleared from the first 7-15 years of my childhood life. I am cleared from everything that I felt and happened from 7-15 years old. I am cleared."

F- Describe and in detail write your life from 15- 18 years old, including all details of your friends, relationships, activities, studies, surroundings, feelings, etc…

G- Scratch what you wrote. Write and audibly say with confidence 10 times:

"I delete the first 15-18 years of my teenage life. I affirm that all events, feelings, thoughts, relationships, people, emotions are 100% cleared from my body, and my mind. I am cleared from the first 15-18 years of my childhood life, and I am clear. I am clear. I am clear."

H- Describe and in detail write your life from 18 years old until today, including details about everything you can think of from material possessions, work, environment, relationships, conflicts, mental and physical blockages, illnesses, sicknesses and so forth.

I- Scratch what you wrote. Write, believe, and audibly say with confidence 10 times:

I delete everything I know, believe, and felt from 18 years old until today. I am cleared from the past. I am a new being open to new thoughts, emotions, feelings and a future that I truly desire. I affirm that I am a new person with a new mind and body. I have a new life, and the full ability to re-design my body and mind. I will master my new self."

You did a great job! Now sometimes, when we wash our clothes, our clothes are not fully washed. Therefore, it is up to you repeat the above exercises until your body, mind, subconscious: accepts, believes, feels that everything is being cleared to a new you. If you still feel that you are carrying more junk, make the next list after the above exercise, and list your negative emotions, beliefs, and thoughts in column format.

1. Negative emotions, Negative Beliefs, Negative Thoughts
2. Re- write, and audibly repeat the exact opposite statement three times.
3. Positive emotions, Positive New Beliefs, Positive Thoughts

4. When you feel a sign of relief, relaxation, trust in yourself, blissfulness, inner connection, peace, and happiness you have truly succeeded in the exercise.

Your new curiosity may re-spark to explore new things and follow your heart's passion. It may take 1-6 months or more 3-5 times daily, but once you have removed all of it you will feel fantastic. Your mind will open up, your body will have less pain, your thoughts will be more creative.

Another alternative to this exercise, is to scratch all your above negative responses from the previous above questions and put them in an envelope.

Seal and write on your envelope:

"I affirm that I am a new being. I am a new being in thought, body, mind, and spirit. I am in control and master myself, my life, and my future. I am protected, guided, and secure. I am blessed, loved, and grateful. I have a beautiful future ahead of me with my passions, desires, and a goal to fulfil. I am worthy of my existence."

Make sure every time that you complete the exercise, you always end by putting all your junk in the envelope, and allocate one minute for a silent release meditation visualizing your new self and life.

Silent Release Meditation

1. From a calm and seated position, close your eyes for 1 minute.
2. Envision for a minute what will your next phase in your life be like. How will you want to look? How will you want to feel? How will you be? What will be your most powerful positive emotions? Where will you live? Who and how will your partner look like and be? Or will you be single?
3. Envision this new you in every detail, and finish your meditation with an affirmation that you believe in it, such as, for example:

    "I believe that I am protected, secure, and loved. Or, I believe that I attract miracles everyday."

4. Your affirmation will only come true when your heart, feeling, and belief are synchronized. If you are short of affirmations, you can purchase the affirmation deck from our website to help you through your meditations.

Well done, now that you have released and freed all or part of your junk, you can begin to practice re-connecting back to nature. Take a walk in the nature, or practice gardening, and explore and keep your presence close to nature and greenery. Everything around you is beautiful, and so are you.

Open your eyes and senses to feel earth, nature, and all that exists within them. Practice the emotion of curiosity, laughter, love, and happiness as you have removed the junk. Your strongest power of change will start from within, and with connection to the higher source of existence and being.

5.   Repeat daily, and re-affirm loudly:

"I affirm I am an amazing human being. I am ready to master myself, and gain full power of my mind, body, and spirit. I am guided by the universe and faith, and trust the higher power. Thank you."

In summary, our suppression, junk and lack of feeling, acting, and being free can physically, emotionally, mentally, and spiritually affect our connection, alignment, and inner power with the universe. One must work on clearing and removing everything that does not serve, or is negative from their inventory, and start a new belief and desire to change, evolve, and re-connect with: joy, love, energy, youthfulness, and playfulness.

CHAPTER 7:

Building a Holistic Mind

The Holistic mind is built primarily from the rewiring of our subconscious mind, the re-connection to our child mind, and the building of a positive and creative mind, while maintaining the wisdom of an adult mind.

"Every child is an artist. The problem is how to remain an artist when they grow up."

-Pablo Picasso

The human mind, is the master control system for your entire body that weighs approximately only around 1.5 Kgs in an adult. The mastery of our mind and all within can change our lives. To build a Holistic mind, we must be aware and expand our knowledge, from Chapter 4, to further understand our: conscious, subconscious, and unconscious mind.

Conscious Mind

The consciousness mind is what allows us to be aware of our external environment and internal state. It performs two tasks: allows us to direct our focus, and to imagine what is not necessarily real. It acts like a scanner, by sensing or perceiving, and triggering a need to react. The scanned information is sent to the unconscious or subconscious mind.

Our consciousness probably began as the directed motion of a hungry self towards a source of food. As a result, this allowed us to survive while our competitors could not or randomly moved to a source of food. If we look at the Trichopax Adhaerens, the simplest known animal and life form, they did not need to have consciousness to get food. They absorbed food and mainly microbes with their underside. Overtime, with evolution, conscious, vision, awareness, and memory were developed to give us a sense of time. Infants develop these skills after 8 months of age. At around 18 months of age, children begin self awareness by looking at their reflection in a mirror and their photos.

In the Holistic mind practices, understanding the way the conscious mind is meant to be used is important because it can significantly change one's reality. One is taught to turn on and off the conscious mind through the Holistic practices. This an extremely powerful tool because it can change our reality, and we can quickly connect and re-connect to different sources of energy and power.

As we have seen from history, the conscious mind was used to gain an awareness of our environment to survive, respond to external threats and get food. Today, our conscious minds are used much more than our subconscious mind, and this affects and impacts our reality, the world's reality, and the future. In the Holistic mind practices and meditations, one is taught how to re-connect to the language that the subconscious understands and builds their reality from it. If our vision is healthy, positive, and happy, our brain chemistry will convert that into our reality. If we live in fear, we are only promoting illness simply because we are not properly aligned with the code and language that the universe understands. It is important that we own our vision as that will create our behaviour and the biology we express in life.

In conclusion, consciousness is a behaviour that is controlled by the brain, and emerges from the need to survive, communicate, play and use tools. It communicates with the external world through self-speech, images, writing, physical movement, and thought. Our conscious mind must be used for their purposes, and we should not live our lives from only our conscious minds to be happy, healthy, and youthful.

The Subconscious Mind

The subconscious mind stores recent things, memories, current thoughts, behavioural patterns, feelings and habits. The subconscious mind's role is to ensure that we react the way we are programmed. For example, if we are present and focused on walking on the sidewalk, our conscious mind will absorb details such as sidewalk signs, rocks, trees and so forth. The moment that we start thinking about something other than walking on the sidewalk, our subconscious mind is working. The majority of us are never really 100% present in the things we do. As a result, science suggests that 95% percent of our life comes from the downloaded programs we get from others, our environment, education and so forth from approximately the first 7 years of our life. Moreover, psychologists believe that the programs implanted in our subconscious mind are mostly dis-empowering or negative. The Holistic therapies and mind practices help re-program the subconscious mind through Holistic meditation, repetition, and energy consultations.

The energy consultations are extremely powerful and life changing. These sessions, due to their high costs, are mostly popular and used by high profile clients and CEO's. These sessions were designed by Julie, and through a kind of Holistic hypnosis clients engage in a higher field of energy. From that field, we work on re-programming our desired visions, events, and circumstances. The results are truly breath taking, and work miracles for those who already have an empowered spiritual connection.

In conclusion, our subconscious mind's job is to act exactly how we have been programmed. It stores our beliefs, past experience, memories, and skills. It can only be re-programmed through Holistic therapies and meditations such as Energy consultations, repetition, hypnotherapy, visualizations.

The Unconscious Mind

The unconscious mind can be thought of as our underground cellar that stores all past trauma, and experiences that we no longer need. Unfortunately, our beliefs, habits, behaviours are formed from here. Sigmund Freud believed change happens when we work with the unconscious mind through psychoanalysis. Freud divided our estimated usage of each level as 10 % conscious, 50-60% subconscious, 30-40% unconscious.

Reprogramming Our Mind

To achieve a Holistic mind, one must understand the subconscious and conscious mind, brain, energy, frequency, vibration, thoughts, emotions, and train the brain repetitively with discipline.

Our minds can be rewired through Holistic meditations and Energy consultation sessions that act similar to hypnosis practice, repetition, and energy psychology. During Holistic meditations and Energy consultation sessions one is connected to a higher field of energy and through the help of a Holistic consultant the mind is rewired. One's energy, vibration, and frequency are raised and aligned with oneself and the universe. To raise our vibration and frequency we must be conscious of it, and careful of our thoughts and words. We must practice the divine language of: gratitude, love, compassion, kindness, honesty, and forgiveness to raise our vibrations. Emotions such as: anger, sadness, jealousy, anxiety, stress, guilt have lower vibrations, and can make us sick. Toxic thoughts, junk foods, substance abuse, negative self-talk, self-sabotaging behaviours, lack of nature exposure, and talking bad of others lower our vibration. In our modern world we must increase our vibrational frequency. The best way to rewire and train our thoughts, beliefs, habits, and behaviour's is to match vibration with the divine frequency and abide to its language. In Chapter 12 we will explore this further.

In the Holistic methodology there are many styles of meditations and practices targeted for different purposes. At the beginner meditation level, students are taught to quiet the mind, learn how to breathe, and gain inner awareness of oneself. At the intermediate level, students experience higher internal and external awareness, vibration, learn different breathing techniques, subconscious communication and re-programming. They will possess ability to meditate for longer durations, visualize and project multiple visualizations, and can easily turn inwards to find inner calmness in mind, body, and energy. At more advanced levels, meditations are used to focus on customized needs such as: healing, abundance, success, energetic fields of force, visualization, eye projections and more. They may require a mentor to work with.

"Watch your thoughts;

They become words.

Watch your words;

They become actions.

Watch your actions;

They become habits.

Watch your habits;

They become character.

Watch you character;

It becomes your destiny."

-Lao Tzu

Building The Holistic Child Mind

A child's mind can be thought of being a new and pure sponge that is curious, creative, imaginative, and receptive to receive and store information. In the Holistic methodology, we strive to connect to our child-like mind when needed and be, feel, and let go as a child to feel happy, energized, and youthful.

A child's sensory system is built during infancy while infants use their primary senses to: touch, taste, see, smell, and hear. Our sensory systems are constantly receiving external input from these senses that create our behaviours. For example, if a child touches something sharp, they will not touch it again because they know it hurts. As our sensory system matures, the brain also develops skills such as interpreting speech, reasoning, movement, emotions, and learning. Unfortunately, as we age, our system does not have a way to remove and clear out negative emotions, experiences, thoughts, because of behaviour, social, and system rules that define who we might be today. For example, a 40 year old yelling on the streets, and having a tantrum may be perceived as abnormal behaviour, while a 3 year old conducting the same behaviour is acceptable. As a result, it is important that we self-clean and purify our emotions, thoughts, feelings as learnt in Chapter 6.

As children get older, they begin to go through the why questioning phase. They always ask why does this or that happen. The act of questioning is an awakening phase, in which children try to gather more information. Questioning is perceived as a great sign of transformation in the Holistic methodology and highly encouraged.

If a mind is stuck or blocked, other Holistic practices are encouraged for clients to engage in to free the mind. Such practices could include: art, dance, connection and observation of nature, poetry, planting, farming, and childlike games, such as: tag, hide and seek, freeze, peek a boo and so forth. As a mind's rusty surface is cleaned, a new mind can be born and developed altogether to be youthful and joyful.

In conclusion, the Holistic mind is reset to achieve awareness and calmness, happiness, joy, positivity, and to create empowering thoughts, beliefs, and actions. The Holistic mind is playful yet mature, curious, energized, and possesses a self- empowering inner-mental system. In the Holistic mind's practices, one is aware of their thoughts, vibration, and energy. These practices focus to improve and rewire the mind by abiding to the universal language of: love, peace, forgiveness, compassion, and kindness.

One should equally engage in Holistic mind, body, and spiritual connection and training to be fully Holistic in body, mind, and soul.

"A Holistic Mind can be true wanders to enhance one's life, body, mind and soul on all levels."

-Julie Rammal

Holistic Mind Exercise

1. Take a deep breath and close your eyes.
2. Think about everything that you know because you experienced it and everything you know because someone told you that.
3. Open your eyes and draw two columns on a piece of paper.
4. In the first column, write everything you know because you experienced it. In the second column, write everything you know because someone else told you that.
5. Review, reflect and compare your responses in column one and two.
6. Practice beginner level meditation to mentally clear the second column.

This can be practiced with a Holistic trainer for more advanced work and results.

Beginner Holistic Meditation

From a comfortable seated position:

1. Close your eyes, and sit in an upright position.
2. Allow your arms to hang freely on the side of your body or place your palms facing upwards on your thighs.

3. Bring your awareness to your breath.

4. Inhale from your nose for 5-10 seconds, pause, and slowly exhale for 10 to 15 seconds.

5. Observe your body, breath, and mind.

6. Focus only on your breath as you sit for 5 to 15 minutes daily, quieting your mind, and continue this meditation for as long as needed to gain inner serenity, awareness, and consciousness of yourself.

Founder Of Holistic Movement, Julie Rammal, Demonstrating The Beginner Meditation.

Beginner Holistic Meditation for Calm Mind

From a seated position:

1. Close your eyes and focus on your breath to calm your mind.

2. Focus deeply on the rise of your inhale, and lengthen your exhales with each round of breath.

3. Visualize seeing the calm version of yourself mirrored in front of you.

4. Notice the relaxed shoulders, facial expressions, and rise and fall of breath.

5. Keep your breath cycle flowing naturally.

6. Perform 5- 15 minutes of meditation, and increase your meditation time with time.

7. When done, smile, and slowly open your eyes.

Beginner Laughing Mind

1. Find an object to observe.

2. Use your creative mind to find something funny about or in it to laugh about, such as: texture, color, shape, taste and so forth.

3. Allow your mind to be free, creative, and to engage in re-experiencing the object through your child's eyes and heart, and laugh with it.

Intermediate Holistic Meditation for Change

From a seated position:

1. Close your eyes and focus on your breath to calm your mind.

2. Allow your exhale to be longer than your inhale.

3. Quiet your mind, relax all of your muscles, while maintaining an upright posture.

4. Take your awareness to your past thoughts, negative beliefs, experiences, traumas, actions, and place them into a small imaginary visualized box during your meditation.

5. Focus on 5 deep inhales and exhales to reset your breath and mind.

6. On your 6th inhale and exhale, envision seeing this small box travelling further away from you until your 10th breath cycle.

7. On your 11th – 15th breath cycle, reset your breath and mind.

8. On your 16th inhale breathe in empowering thoughts, emotions, beliefs, and visualizations that you would like to have and see for yourself.

9. Focus on them until your 20th breath cycle.

10. Continue naturally inhaling and exhaling until you mentally, emotionally and physically feel this little negative box is no longer connected to you and you have grown your new empowering thoughts, emotions, beliefs, and visualization in a new larger box.

11. To close your meditation, take a deep inhale and exhale for 3 rounds of breath, and re affirm your new box: empowering thoughts, emotions, beliefs, and visualization.

12. Slowly open your eyes, smile, and say thank you to the universe.

Holistic Meditation for Mind & Subconscious Mind

From a seated position:

1. Close your eyes and focus on your breath to calm your mind.

2. Allow your mind to be completely calm.

3. Naturally breathing in and out, envision seeing your mind and subconscious mind in front of you.

4. In front of you, your conscious mind floats like a small balloon under your larger subconscious balloon.

5. Take a few more deep breaths focusing on this visualization, as your subconscious balloon is physically expanding with every breath.

6. Place a label on your subconscious mind of what you desire. It could be prosperity, peace, success, love, happiness etc… and label it with your desire. For example, "I am happy, I am successful, I have a loving relationship, and so forth."

7. Audibly tell yourself that you believe in what you have just stated and labelled your subconscious balloon with.

8. Re-affirm it several times from your heart with feeling and emotion.

9. Repeat your belief affirmations several times with true feeling.

10. Once you have labelled your message on the subconscious balloon, continue to breathe, delete any negative thoughts, images, memories, experiences that try to enter your mind.

11. Take a few deep breaths focusing on the large subconscious label.

12. As you connect with the large subconscious balloon and label, see, feel, and visualize everything that reflects the label you have placed on the balloon. For example, if you labelled your subconscious balloon as I am happy, visualize seeing everything that is happy in your world and yourself.

13. To end your meditation, take 3 deep grounding breaths, and slowly open your eyes thanking the universe for your practice.

14. After any Holistic meditation, it is always a great practice to end your meditation with the Beginner Laughing Mind exercise. As such, you will keep your creative mind open, youthful; and generate creativity, change of perception, happiness, and feeling. If you are practicing Holistic group meditations, sharing a friendly hug or a simple laugh with the person near you is also a great way to share and expand energy.

"A day without laughter, is a day wasted."
-Charlie Chaplin

To empower your meditations, you can purchase the self-transformation deck from www,holisticmovement.co for empowering thoughts, beliefs, energy and vibration. Additional complimentary YouTube meditations are also available on YouTube: Holistic Movement Julie Rammal, or through our training section on our website.

In conclusion, once one has mastered and practiced the Holistic meditative practices, they can re-generate renewed thoughts, beliefs, perceptions, and visualizations through their mind. A Holistic mind is calm, aware, contains empowering thoughts, beliefs, and is childlike in imagination yet wise like an adult mind.

With advanced meditation practices, our meditation can be completed with the <u>Three arm circle exercise</u> described in Chapter 5 and 11. One must master the ability to shut down the mind and open the subconscious mind to feel energy, joy, and connection between themselves and the universe.

"A Holistic Mind generates a Holistic and healthy life."

-Julie Rammal

C H A P T E R   8 :

Building a Holistic Body

A Holistic body, is a child's body before any mental, physical, emotional blockages occur. The Holistic methodology focuses on removing all blockages to find a naturally balanced, strong, energized, healthy, and youthful body. To achieve a Holistic body, the Holistic methodology reprograms the body by removing blockages from negative emotions, tension, and retrains our motor skills, precision, control, coordination, endurance, flexibility, and natural breath and strength through movements that our body recognizes and reacts to.

"A Holistic body is a child's body with adult intelligence in: awareness, control, balance, strength, breath, flexibility and discipline."

-Julie Rammal

To understand the Holistic body, we must understand how our body changes and progresses from childhood to elderly years, and the movements that our body recognizes to make us feel: happy, energized, and youthful. Through understanding we can be aware, re-program and rewire our body back to natural homeostasis.

Development of Body in Infants

During an infant's early years, infants move in certain ways to build postural muscles, and fine and gross motor skills. The use of smaller muscles allow their motor skills to: grab, reach, hold small objects, use fingers and wrists, button clothing, turn pages etc.. The gross motor skills require large muscle usage to enable babies to: crawl, lift head, roll over, sit and stand up, touch toes, walk, balance, climb, jump and so forth. During baby's tummy time, babies develop their core and postural muscles. Postural muscles affect a child's attention, focus, breath, and other movements. Later on, babies learn to roll from their back to their belly. As they master these skills, they learn to sit, hold their own head and body weight, and then develop the skill of crawling. Crawling helps strengthen the primary basic muscles of children such as: stomach, back, neck, legs, and arms.

The Holistic body honours the infant's muscular growth cycle, and combines the basics of movement with exercises, to tone each muscle in the body naturally with: awareness, breath, flow, control and discipline.

Adults Body

The adult body usually matures at around 18 years old and continuously changes as one ages. At the age of around 30, the skin loses elasticity, wrinkles appear, muscles may lose strength, and eye sight can degrade. In addition, as one ages, ligaments start to shorten, joints stiffen, cartilage thins, and flexibility is lost. Emotional, mental, and physical blocks start to accumulate creating generally a blocked body that is filled with emotions of: fear, lack or over confidence, trauma, stress and more. The mental, emotional, and physical blocks continue to increase with age causing less movement, decreased range of motion, lack of flexibility, lethargy, slower speed, less balance, coordination and more negative emotions. They key to reversing all of this is by using the Holistic methodology movement system to create a balance, happy, energized, and youthful body. The Holistic methodology is anti-aging, and its success lies in moving correctly with a language that our bodies understand.

Middle to Elderly Age Body

By adult to middle age the body usually selects what it physically or habitually likes to do. For example, each sport, movement, thought, action, emotion, and behaviour impact how our body looks like, even though we all have the same bodily form. Our movement becomes a reflection of where we are in our lives, and our connection to ourselves.

One can visibly notice that the shape and performance of different bodies engaged, in different body movements, look and function differently, such as: ballet, dance, basketball, football, body building, boxing, gym, gymnastics, yoga, Pilates, or martial arts, etc.. Each of these bodies have different appearances and skills such as: speed, power, control, discipline, endurance, flexibility and strength. The way one moves can tell a lot about one's identity and how one thinks and behaves.

At approximately 40 years and onwards, additional physical changes continue to persist such as: cardiac output decreases, higher blood pressure, decrease in flexibility, respiratory flow rates slow down, breath shortens, skin loses elasticity and thins, bones and muscles weaken, pains and injuries may begin to occur and so forth.

The Holistic methodology strives to bring all major sport disciplines together, through: mastery, awareness, training, and discipline of our body, and in a language that it understands and reacts to.

The Holistic methodology can re-balance a human body to its original root shape and create youthful, flexible, energized, and natural toned figures. The Holistic Movement helps the human body to act, behave youthfully and vibrantly while maintaining a balanced, flexible, unblocked, and strong physical structure at any age. The Holistic methodology's exercises and movements are specifically designed to understand and honour the body. For example, the movements move harmoniously with the body's code of movement, and focus to naturally lengthen and strengthen our: muscles, joints, and overall body to give us a profound posture and stance.

In conclusion, the Holistic body is formed when we remove all mental, physical, emotional blockages and expand our oneness with the outer space and universe. As a result, our senses are dramatically improved alongside with: speed, alertness, fluidity, concentration, discipline, endurance, precision, flexibility, and joint and muscle functions. With the power and connection to our Holistic body, we can heal, tone, manage weight, improve our intuitiveness, manifest things, and gain immense powers. We learn the true power of the human body, and help excel it to reach its natural abilities and potentials.

Holistic Body Movement and Emotion

The Holistic movement recognizes the language of the body, and works with it to release, re-balance, and realign itself freely to a higher source of power. The more our bodies are emotionally and physically free, the happier we automatically feel because this what the body desires most.

If we look back at our childhood years, there are certain movements that we used to do that made us feel and react to in a certain way. If these movements are repeated at present, or at an older age, our body quickly recognizes the emotion and past movements, and begins to act and feel the way it used to with practice. For example, if we skip, this movement produces endorphins which make us feel happier and less stressed. Children who skip often laugh or smile because it is a movement that our body identifies as freedom and happiness. If we sit or stand tall and confidently, we automatically feel better because our bodies love to be beautiful and alive. Dancing is also another wonderful movement that expresses feeling and emotions, and makes one feels great.

Our movements are a wonderful way to connect and detoxify our bodily system to feel better, improve health, awareness, blood flow, naturally tone and re-connect within ourselves.

Holistic Body Levels

A Holistic body is built in three levels, beginner, intermediate, advanced, and can take months to over 15 years to master. The advancement from each level depends on how much baggage one is carrying in terms of: blockages, disrupted breath patterns, past injuries/ surgeries, stress, fear, traumas, physical history and background, vision, will power, body, and mindset. Movements are never forced upon the body, but gradually introduced and joined with the body when it begins to demonstrate signs of: openness, change, trust, and ability.

Holistic Movement sessions are encouraged to practice 2- 5 times a week to build a strong consistent foundation, and to develop and regrow the body correctly in a movement that our bodies understand and naturally adapt to. It is important to note that, from past experience, most beginner students are mentally, physically and emotionally unaligned, and if not properly guided they may quickly give up. Many beginner students come with the mindset that they will come in the first session and do all of the exercises easily. However; the reality is that in the first 15-20 minutes, the beginner student is fatigued and stops. The reason behind this is because the body, mind and emotions are not trained nor aligned and are holding onto heavy blockages on all levels. The body may still be suffering from trauma, stress, negative past events, fatigue etc., while the mind is pushing the body forward to succeed.

The Holistic methodology works on adapting the workout to the bodies status and never forces the body for something it is not ready for. The body is respected and gently trained and challenged, at a pace allowing it to continue training for life.

The Holistic methodology works on bringing the: body, mind, and soul into awareness and balance, while training and disciplining each equally through various advancements in each level. The study and training of breath advances through each level. In Chapter 9, we will learn more about the power of breath.

"Without breath, there is no movement, as breath gives the body, mind and soul life."
-Julie Rammal

Level 1 - Beginner: The beginner student learns the classic Holistic warm up and basic exercises to move, breath, focus, train, and discipline the outside physical shell. Students learn how to naturally move again with their own weight as an infant, and gain a basic awareness of their body. Beginners build the fundamental building blocks for: muscle tone, flexibility, removing muscle and joint blockages, and building natural strength. The postural muscles of abdominals, back, neck, legs, and upper body begin training at basic level 1 exercises.

The Beginner level offers a basic inner and external awareness of the self, breath, control and awakening of all body limbs, and basic Holistic meditation is also conducted. Generally, the maximum number of repetitions per exercise is limited to 10.

Level 2 - *Intermediate*: Once the Holistic body masters all level 1 concepts, it spends most of its time training in Level 2 to be more alert, aware, and ready to grow, and be physically and mentally challenged with: speed, endurance, power, fluidity, breath, movement, discipline, focus, strength, and coordination. Blockages are continuously worked on to increase flexibility, and the body can sit in stillness for longer timeframes. At this level, more advanced movements and routines are given to challenge: balance, coordination, postural, abdominal, back, neck, legs, and upper body strength and flexibility. A student's state of mind can be improved during Holistic meditations, as communication with subconscious is easily understood.

At Level 2, student gain awareness of their soul, and start to feel and communicate with their inner systems, such as: heart, thoughts, emotions, and breath. Exercises can be performed repetitively and consistently without a break. Balance, coordination, awareness, control, breath, flexibility, discipline, and natural strength are well grasped and practiced. The inner-self is intermediately fulfilled with an expanding external universal alignment. Lastly, at an intermediate level, repetitions may increase to 20-30.

Level 3 - *Advance*: The Holistic body is physically aware, alert, and balanced in body, mind, and soul with the outside space energy or universe. One's five senses of smell, sight, feeling, hearing, and touch are highly developed. Despite the Holistic body's calmness, it is fast, strong, flexible, powerful, full of endurance when needed and yet tranquil. At this level, the body masters the 5 Chinese elements philosophy and can quickly transfer from one to the other.

At the Advance Level, all concepts of Levels 1 and 2 are 100% grasped. The body is physically and emotionally balanced, mentally disciplined, controlled, trained, and has high awareness, speed, control, endurance, strength, flexibility, power and visualization. The Holistic body can perform with ease: dance, basic fight movement, Holistic exercises and sequences, balance, coordination, flexibility, flow, power and strength, meditation, and basics of recovery and healing. Various advanced routines are performed, and a stronger inner communication within and outside of the self is achieved at ease. The Holistic body experiences various levels of mediation and can direct breath to each body part. The basics of recovery and self-healing are addressed.

For a body to become Holistically self-independent and self-sufficient, it must complete and master all 3 levels at ease. At the same time, individuals can use the whole Holistic methodology to train, or select certain parts that interest them such as: upper body strength, core, meditation, flexibility, etc…

Finally, only a few students are able to pursue their training further, to attain super human powers such as: seeing auras, chakras, organs, energy, telepathy, and can easily project: healing, manifestations, energy and field projections, change in heart and body temperature using mind and breath, 3rd eye opening, and more.

"The Holistic methodology is the body code movement to reach success and discipline."

-Julie Rammal

Supported Body Movements For the Body

The Holistic methodology encourages natural movements to propel training, awareness, weight management, breath, coordination, power, speed, strength and more. The Holistic methodology encourages trainees to engage in natural outdoor activities, such as: walking, jogging, running, dancing, stretching, martial arts, gymnastics. All movements are also supported in moderation and encouraged for advancement.

In conclusion, the Holistic body is a temple and reflection of ourselves. We should treat our body with care, love, and feed it with breath, positivity, healthy organic foods, music and sound, and build our internal communication with our systems while training it with awareness, discipline, focus, breath, consistency, speed, power, strength and control.

"When our bodies are enlightened with training, each one of us will shine brighter."

-Julie Rammal

CHAPTER 9:

Building a Holistic Breath

Our breath is the first thing that acknowledges we are alive, and the moment we cut it off we are slowly dis-connecting and unknowingly dying.

Our breath is a source of inner life within ourselves, and a connection to the physical and spiritual world. The power of the Holistic breath can decrease anxiety, depression, stress, improves respiratory health, focus, stamina, concentration, and mental state to process emotions, thoughts, and vision.

"The Holistic breath can take one to another dimensional plane of existence in body and mind."

-Julie Rammal

Our breath is conducted in two simple phases, inspiration and exhalation. Our inhalations cause our intercostal muscles and diaphragm to contract creating a vacuum effect. When we exhale, our lungs contract to force air out of the lungs.

The power of breath has many secrets that can change how we feel, think, perceive, our health, and move energy. Moreover; breath gives us control over our body and mind. During meditation, the breath and the use of symbols are used to empower our meditation practices, by centering our focus, bringing awareness, and re-connecting to a higher source of power. In this respect, one of the most powerful symbols that may be used in meditation is the Sri Yantra and Mandala symbol.

In the Holistic methodology, breath is regarded as a source to life and a higher connection to oneself and to the spiritual world. Breath is equally trained with mind and body practices. In the Holistic methodology we focus primarily on the basic natural breath flow of breath that new born and children have. The breath naturally expands during inhalation, and during exhalation it naturally contracts with a slight and natural expansion and contraction in belly movement. Our Holistic breath is focused and trained to be natural, unforced, and to flow naturally within us. The benefits of this breath include improved blood flow, energy, posture, detoxification, lymphatic system stimulation, digestion, while reducing pain, anxiety, stress, depression, and inflammation.

Our Current Breath

The majority of people breathe in short breath cycles. Breathing in short breath cycles jeopardizes our health and unbalances our body and mind while affecting our chakra, overall energy, emotions, and well-being. The majority of people also live in a stress flight or fright zone, collecting negative emotions such as: stress, worry, fear, sadness, and anger that impact our lower chakra and energy system. If our lower chakra systems are blocked, our relation with the external world, and our physical and emotional self are also affected.

According to the World Health Organization in 2018, 9 in 10 people breathe polluted air, and approximately 7 million people will die from inhaled exposure that disturbs their lungs, and cardiovascular system. In 2020 the coronavirus disease affected millions worldwide leaving many of those who recovered with a permanent lung damage. The rise in pollution, stress, and negative emotions, naturally makes our lungs not want to breathe correctly, and as a result poses a high risk to our overall and respiratory health, and the future of our breath.

One must build a natural breath cycle with conscious awareness for health. Increasing risks in heart disease, illnesses, and chronic obstructive pulmonary diseases and respiratory infections will continue to rise if we do not learn and connect to the natural way of breath. We should give life to every breath, and feel a sense of inner calmness, peace, gratitude, and happiness with every breath we take.

We must increase our connection to the human race and re-connect ourselves to our higher energy sources. Our higher energy centers include feelings of trust in the universe, faith, and love. If our higher energy centers are connected with the Divine field, our lower energy centers that are governed by: fear, anxiety, grudges, addictions, manipulation, suppression, and negative emotions, will naturally dissolve.

We can lift our higher energy centers by practicing the Holistic Methodology and the Holistic Code of conduct and beliefs discussed in Chapter 2 with meditation, eating healthy and balanced foods, and being connected and living in harmony with the universe.

> *"Natural breath can re-connect the human race to rise in a new dimensional plane of existence where peace, love, serenity and calmness exist."*
>
> -Julie Rammal

In order to change our breath, we must re-connect to our natural breath cycles to activate our higher chakras, such as the heart and crown chakra. The power and awareness of our breath can transfer energy into other parts of our body, improve our health, state of consciousness and inner and external connection to the universe.

"The human breath gives rise to humanity."
-Julie Rammal

It is no wonder that the majority of us suffer from pain, lack of happiness, social bonding, reproduction problems and more. If we breathe properly, then our breath can alter negative emotions, and produce Oxytocin - the love chemical, and endorphins - the calming and analgesic effect.

In conclusion, a natural breath is the body's first remedy to joy, healthy, body and mind balance to build a strong internal harmonious self, filled with energy and vibration. Our breath must be harmonized with our heart and aligned with the natural universal flow of breath. By building on the power of our natural breath, we can resolve most of our health problems, experience positive emotions, love, calmness, and enrich our connection with the spirit world to download and receive visions, improve intuitiveness and connection.

The Holistic Breath

In the Holistic methodology, we focus on only one breath, the natural breath that a child and new born have, because it is what life gave to every human. Our breath is practiced repetitively with consistency and discipline until it is mastered to be a natural action or behaviour without effort. When we join breath with movement, we are more interconnected, aligned, aware, free, and conscious of our body, mind and spirit. We grow deeper within ourselves, all of our systems, and create a bond with the Divine field.

The Holistic methodology focuses on one basic style of breath, because people are born with this breath, and everything around us follows the same cycle of our natural breath. For example, everything rises and falls, such as: sunset/sunrise, sleeping/awakening, action/resting, and so forth. The power of natural breath improves our connection to ourselves and the universe, allowing us to gain inner peace, and happiness. By changing the length and duration of our natural breath, we could alter our state of consciousness, focus, move energy, and change our mood during movement or meditation.

Holistic Breath Exercise

To practice the Holistic breath:

1. Sit comfortably on a chair with your legs a few inches apart, and arms to the side of your hips or place palms facing upward on the top of your thighs.

2. Inhale naturally expand your belly for a few seconds, pause for 2-3 seconds, and naturally exhale slightly contracting your belly inwards. The rise of inhale and fall of exhale should be similar in duration and not forced but move harmoniously within.

3. Practice for 5-10 minutes daily to gain a natural tendency to breathe correctly.

Holistic Breath & Pineal Gland Activation

1. From a comfortable seated position, close your eyes, and place arms at the side of hips or palms facing upward on thighs.

2. Begin the Holistic breath for 3-5 minutes. As you breathe, focus your attention and awareness on the center between your eyebrows to begin bringing energy and awareness to this area. Imagine a golden beam of light enter this center point as your breath. With each breath, the golden beam of light taps deeper into your 3rd eye point. Focus on your 3rd eye point and feel the sensations, pulsations, or shift in tension as you breathe into this point.

3. Continue breathing in without any expectation and feeling your natural breath rise and fall for another 1-2 minutes. When done, open your eyes.

4. If you were unable to open your 3rd eye continue practicing, and if you were able to open it you may receive messages from other awakened beings as you connect to this high energy point.

Be aware that opening the 3rd eye point is a beautiful and new experience, however; some people may experience unsettling experiences, headaches, tension, initiate their ability to see people's auras, experience a series of awakenings, and initiation of an entirely new level of social interactions

Sri Yantra & Holistic Breath Meditation

The Sri Yantra symbol dates back to around 10,000 years BP, and is one of the earliest sacred geometry that was used in the Shri Vidya school of Hinduism.

The Sri Yantra symbol consists of 9 interlocking triangles that surround a central point. These triangles represent the universe and the human body.

The Sri Yantra shape consists of the external square, in Vedic sacred geometry represents Earth, negative and disturbing emotions and energy such as: fear, anger, worry and so forth. Yogis meditate on this outer square to remove and combat the negative disturbing energies.

The T shape structures in the squares are perceived as the gates to the four directions, and entry points to the yantra, or deity. It can be used for certain benefits such as: meditation, certain powers, health, abundance, or protection from harmful influences.

Sri Yantra

The three circles signify past, present, and future. Within the first circle, there are 16 lotus petals which represent: fulfilment of hopes and desires. The 16 petals represent the mind that collects and interprets information from the perception of the interactivity of the five elements: earth, water, air, fire, and space. The second circle has 8 petals which govern specific activity such as: communication, movement, attraction, and calmness. In the last circle, there are sets of interlocked triangles. The triangles that point upwards represent the masculine principle; and downward facing triangles represent the feminine.

At the lowest outer triangle, moving counterclockwise, there is: worry, quest, attraction, pleasure, misconception, stillness, release, control, intoxication, and acquirement of desire, luxury, and the destruction of duality.

The next circle has the same sequence and direction, starting from the lowest triangle and moving counterclockwise.

1st triangle: The giver of all accomplishments

2nd triangle: The giver of wealth

3rd triangle: The energy of activities that please all

4th triangle: The supplier of blessings

5th triangle: The granter of all desires

6th triangle: The remover of all suffering

7th triangle: The pacifier of death

8th triangle: The overcomer of all obstacles.

9th triangle: The provider of beauty

10th triangle: The donor of all good fortune.

The ten smaller triangles in the third circle represent, beginning at the same, lowermost triangle and moving counterclockwise: knowledge, omnipotence, power, wisdom, destruction of all disease, unconditional support, removal of all evils, protection, and the attainment of all desires.

The fourth circle of triangles, starting at the same point and moving counterclockwise, represent: sustaining, creating, termination, pleasure, pain, and the ability to choose action.

In the final inner space, the yogi or meditator visualizes five arrows, where each part of the arrow signifies senses. A bow - the mind, the noose – attachment, and a stick - aversion. The central triangle is the giver of all perfection, and within it a dot called Bindu, which represents our original state of being and pure consciousness. The Bindu is the highest manifestation of the deity, and a point where the deity transcends to the relative plane, and forms a formless consciousness.

The central dot in the Bindu is the symbol of AUM, which is the final stage, or as earlier learnt from previous chapters, the first sound of the universe. The Sri Yantra reveals the potential nature of the devotee to merge in a loving relationship with the Divine as the divine.

Finally, the Sri Yantra symbol is very powerful. In 1987, Russian scientists proved that the Sri Yantra symbol rapidly brings viewers to a meditative state using EEG technology.

Basic Meditation, Breath & Sri Yantra

Through meditation, we can bring the geometry in our consciousness. To do so:

1. Select a handmade copper Sri Yantra or if unavailable you can make your own Sri Yantra or use the black and white Sri Yantra image.

2. Place your Sri Yantra against a white surface, such as a wall, in front of you at eye height. It should not be above your head or below your navel. Before you begin, remember that the Sri Yantra symbol represents our divinity point.

3. Connect back to your natural Holistic breath as you softly gaze at the image for 5 minutes.

4. After 5 minutes, quickly gaze at a white blank surface. You will see the black and white Sri Yantra image until it starts to slowly fade away.

5. Once it disappears, close your eyes, breathe in naturally, and allow all remaining after images to emerge until all is faded.

6. Practice daily for 30 days, and notice the changes that may sprout in your life.

Intermediate Basic Meditation, Breath & Sri Yantra for Desires

Whatever you desire or chose to bring in into your life, you can begin to focus on in your meditations for 20 minutes a day.

For example, for health, happiness or a relationship:

1. Meditate for 20 minutes, focusing on the bindu dot daily for 30 days and re-affirming what you have received.

2. After 20 minutes of meditation, you can enrich your practice by visualizing, and feeling what you have affirmed.

Draw Your Sri Yantra

Another powerful way to use your Sri Yantra is make one yourself, versus just getting a printed symbol. Everything that is designed and created by our hands has a different effect and power on us and our relation to it. To draw the basics of our Sri Yantra you will need a compass, ruler, pencil, and eraser. Follow the below steps, and pay attention to the accuracy, alignment and distances.

Draw Your Sri Yantra

Step 1: Draw a large circle following the approximate distance range.

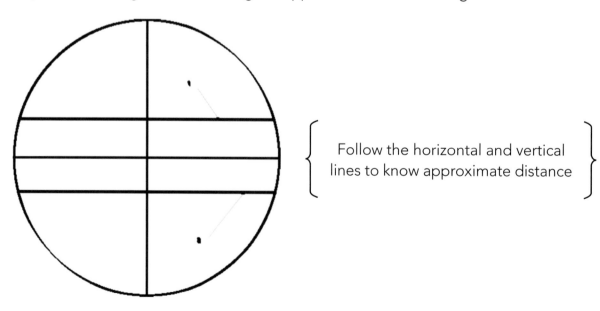

Follow the horizontal and vertical lines to know approximate distance

Step 2: Draw 2 reverse triangles in the circle

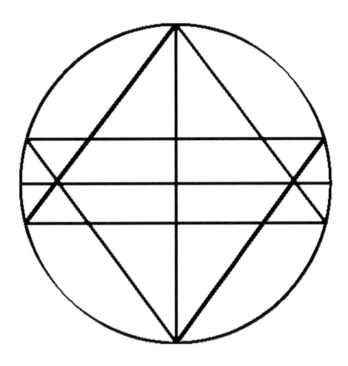

Step 3: Draw 2 more reverse triangles in the circle

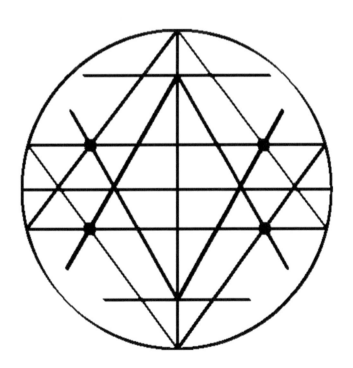

Step 4: Continue drawing the opposite direction of triangles, until you reach 4 downward pointing triangles, and 5 upward pointing triangles, and it should look like the following image.

Step 5: In the final inner triangle, draw a circle with a pencil, and place a dot in the middle of it to signify the Bindu point. Erase the drawn circle.

Mandala & Holistic Breath Meditation

A mandala represents the spiritual journey within the individual viewer. A mandala is a symbolic image of the cosmos that originated in Buddhism and was created in the 4th century. Its purpose was to transform ordinary minds, enlighten them, and promote healing.

Mandala

Mandala Floral Flower Abstract

The mandala was produced in Tibet, India, Nepal, China, Japan, Bhutan, Indonesia and today are available worldwide. In Sanskrit, mandala means "circle," and represents the circles of life. This circular form represents the continuity of the universe.

In Yoga the mandala is viewed as unity of body mind and soul. The geometric shapes and configuration of symbols in the mandala can reveal the truths from the universe and those inside your own spirit.

The mandala helps focus meditation and create an induction of trance during meditation. Carl Jung described a mandala as "a representation of the unconscious self."

The mandala and Sri Yantra are similar yet different. The Sri Yantra is a sort of mandala, and similar to it with geometric patterns. The Sri Yantra is a principal, while a mandala is an expression and a geometric patterned plan that represents the universe. The Sri Yantra is a tool for wealth, material, and spiritual abundance. The mandala helps with healing and making one whole, while lifting their inner spirit and wisdom.

To further understand the difference between a Sri Yantra and mandala, think of your life as a mandala, and your DNA as the yantra.

Buddhist monks create a mandala and in the mandala ceremony then they pray and meditate. At the end of the ceremony the mandala is destroyed by the monks because they believe that nothing is eternal, and everything is always moving towards enlightment and balance in life.

In the Holistic meditation, the mandala is used in meditation, prayer, healing and to bring the mind into a balanced state. Many clinical studies have proved that mandalas have the power to boost immunity, reduce pain, stress, lower blood pressure, decrease anxiety and depression. Healing with the mandala can be enhanced by drawing colors and adding an intention in the mandala.

Mandala color and meanings

1. Red: Strength, energy, passion
2. Pink: Love, femininity, intuition
3. Orange: Creativity, intuition, transformation
4. Yellow: Wisdom, learning, laughter, happiness
5. Green: Healing, nature, caring
6. Blue: Emotional healing, communication, inner serenity
7. Purple: Spiritual connection
8. Black: Mystery, individuality, deep thought

Holistic Breath and Mandala Meditation

1. Find a mandala that resonates with you or use the below Mandala to color intuitively with crayon or colored pencils.
2. Set your intention on your mandala when you are done.
3. Sit down in a comfortable position facing your mandala and focus on your intention.
4. Take several deep Holistic breaths as you look at your mandala.
5. Gaze at your mandala until the images become out of focus.

6. Meditate on the center of your mandala for 5 minutes. The geometric shapes will balance your mind. After 5 minutes you will gain a sense of peace, relaxation, and increase your intuitive thoughts.

7. Perform this meditation daily as you build up your meditation practice to 20 minutes daily.

Mandala Pattern For Coloring

"The dream is the small hidden door in the deepest and most intimate sanctum of the soul, which opens into that primeval cosmic night that was soul long before there was a conscious ego and will be soul far beyond what a conscious ego could ever reach."

-Carl Gustav Jung (Discovered while worked with mandala's

In conclusion, breath, and symbols such as the Sri Yantra and Mandala are very powerful during one's spiritual journey and transformation. The Sri Yantra and mandala are designed with powerful geometric shapes. They give us more in-depth awareness of ourselves and how the world works.

"Use breath in everything and everywhere you go, as breath is our primary action upon birth and it should be honoured."

-Julie Rammal

Chapter 10:

Building a Holistic Soul

Ancient religions and the Holistic Movement believe that we have a soul, an immortal part of us that is invisible and embodies our physical, astral and casual bodies.

Our physical body is tangible, as we can see our arms, legs, chest, torso, face and so forth. Our astral bodies can be thought of as an aura or light that surrounds our physical body. Our casual body is the highest body that reveals the soul and has no shape.

Today, the science community does not believe that there is enough evidence to support that a soul exists. The closest scientific documentation of the soul was conducted by Boston Physician Dr. Duncan MacDougall who hypothesized that the soul weighs around 21 grams.

There are many beliefs of how our soul originated or if it really does exist in various dynasties and cultures. In brief, Buddhists do not believe in a soul, but believe in impermanence, an energy being reborn. In Sikhism, the soul is believed to be a part of the Divine. Christians believe that the soul is judged by God after death, and it will either go to heaven or hell. Muslims believe that the soul departs from the physical body after death and continues on to an afterlife. In Islam, it is believed that we have the immortal soul (Ruh) and the mortal soul (Nafs). In other ancient religions, humans are thought of as being souls, and our souls continue on after our physical body dies. The Greeks believed after death that the soul continues on a journey called the underworld. In Plato's book Phaedrus, he demonstrated the immortality of the soul after physical bodily death. In ancient Egypt, the Egyptians believed that the world and everything in it, including human beings, was instilled with magic. That magic and eternal forces was believed to take form as the soul. They believed in the Akh, and the five fragments of the human soul that comprised the Ren, Sheut, Ib, Ba, Ka. The Akh is the physical body and includes the body, Ba, Ka, Ren, and shadow. When one died, the Akh was believed to reunite with the Ba and Ka. The Ren was the birth name given to a person while the Sheut was a person's shadow. The Ib was the metaphysical heart (emotion, thought, intention, will), the Ba was everything that made a person's unique personality for example their charm, warmth, and humor, and the Ka was the vital fire that differentiated living people from dead. The ancient Egyptians believed that when someone died, the soul split into two parts the Ba and the Ka. Every morning the Ba would leave to watch over your existing family, while the Ka would enjoy another life, and in the evening both the Ba and Ka would return to one's tomb to rest for the next day. The ancient Egyptian tombs mummified the bodies to preserve them and gave the tombs a name plate on one's coffin called a cartouche. The cartouche was important for the Ba and Ka to find their way back home. If one did not have a cartouche, the Ba and Ka were believed to get lost, and one would not be able to watch over their family and enjoy one's afterlife. In addition, the mummification of the body was believed to have been done for the soul to reunite with the body after its burial. If the soul could not recognize the body, it would not live forever. The process of body mummification has been practiced in many civilizations in Iran, China, Siberia, Philippines, Denmark, Hungary, Italy, Greenland, ancient Europe, and seen in the Incan, Australian Aboriginal, Aztec, and African civilizations.

In brief, our soul consists of our mental abilities to be a living being with character, feeling, consciousness, memory, perception, thinking and so forth, and can be mortal or immortal depending on various philosophical systems. Our soul may be a mystery and something that each one should scrutinize further to find their own answer.

"Soul loss is regarded as the most serious diagnosis and the single greatest cause of premature death and serious illness by the Traditionals and it's not even mentioned in our Western medical textbooks."

- Deepak Chopra

In the Holistic methodology, one is left to believe one's personal belief on the soul. However, after cross research of ancient beliefs and personal experience, it is believed that we do have a soul. In the Holistic movement exercise, the 3 arm circle, conducted at the end of a session or class, our arms are equally raised and circled backwards in honour and connection to our body, mind and soul. Our soul and our connection to it is what gives us a spark of joy, happiness, and wholeness connection to ourselves. Our souls are a vibration of the divine that contain: truth, peace, love, healing, and abundance.

Our Soul's Today

The majority of people are not connected to their soul, nor its vibration, and are mostly experiencing soul loss or rupture, or are even selling their souls.

The pain that our souls are facing today is rising. It will continue to rise if we do not stop and re-connect to how we are internally designed and honour our code of creation and being. If we do not live from our soul, eventually we become dis-connected from it, and attract our own soul loss and rupture symptoms, where joy may fade and become non-existent. Overtime, with a lack of awareness and care for our soul, we attract negative emotions, experiences, bigger traumas that start to tear more pieces of our soul, and we lose our spark. Each negative, traumatic experience, or shock to our body and mind take a part of our soul away. The easiest way to visualize the power of our soul is to think of the soul as the electricity to a light bulb that gives it light. Symptoms of soul loss are: often manifested in a feeling of emptiness, broken, stuck, incomplete, long periods of insomnia, addictions, co-dependency, eating disorders, memory loss, loss of eye or smile brightness, lack of energy, depression, missing or hurt heart, fear and anxiety.

To change the condition of our soul, one must holistically approach it by returning back to the soul vibration and presence. We should honour and equally treat it as part of who we are. When we are connected and live from our soul, we will experience: joy, happiness, clear mind, feeling of wholeness, and life becomes more beautiful.

Cultivating a Healthy Soul

There are many ways to cultivate our soul, however; as everything we must first have an awareness and belief that we have a soul. Once this is established, one can begin nurturing Holistic meditations or private consultations that focus on balancing body, mind, soul, and empower: self-love, positivity, and re-connection to oneself.

The easiest way to begin re-connecting to our soul is to feel and connect with its needs. One can begin to meditate, read, exercise, love oneself and others unconditionally, practice gratitude and forgiveness, re-connect to nature and oneself, be positive, and do things that make us feel happier and more alive. As such, we should distance ourselves from negative or harmful actions, thoughts, energy, environments, and beliefs until the soul is healed and re-connected to. In Chapter 13, we scrutinize the power of attitude, which is important because our positive attitudes give us power to re-connect back to our soul, let go of ego, and remove old negative habits that take us away from our root being.

In conclusion, one should practice self-reflection, and take time to let go of old and negative things that do not serve the soul's well-being. Engage in positive supportive relations, spend time in nature, read inspirational books and films, do things that give joy; write and journal all feelings, emotions, hopes, desires; and practice holistic breathing, movement, and meditation.

Knowing the Soul's Purpose

The majority of our souls are suffering, ruptured, and de-attached from us. As we get vacuumed into life, we may over ride our soul, and build negative ego, experiences, boundaries, and box ourselves in a world that may be away from our mission, and life purpose. It is very important to stay connected to our soul's purpose and to know our calling in this life.

We can discover our calling when we remove distractions, spend time alone, silence the mind, and start Holistic meditations to connect with our soul's purpose. When we quiet our mind and master meditation, the answer to our soul's purpose will be given to us if repetitively ask what is our soul's purpose. Once we follow our soul's calling, life will move more harmoniously and we will gain our true vision and intuition on our life maze. Consequently, things will start to actualize with less effort and struggle, and we will feel like we are sailing calmer seas.

The Secrets of the Soul

The soul has numerous powers that can enrich our life such as: life, joy, creativity, intuition, and connection to the divine. We can activate our soul's power of creation through higher frequency and vibration, positive thoughts, attitudes, beliefs, gratitude, forgiveness, kindness, open heart, unconditional love, eating light, and practicing the holistic methods.

Our soul holds divine wisdom, knowledge, and practices to alter the human consciousness, and enlighten the human race to spread: peace and love for our world and the universe. In the 20th century and beyond, our connection to our soul will help transform our lives and the human race.

The best way to access our soul's powers is to regularly meditate and exercise, and to listen to the 432 Hertz and 528 Hertz frequencies to create positive resonance and harmony in our cells, DNA, and self. These frequencies will help remove blocked energy flow to create a positive state of mind. When we live at these frequencies, we start to remove or reject negative beliefs, fears, doubts, worries because such frequencies do not resonate with the high positive frequencies of the soul.

The 432 Hz frequency is the magical hertz frequency of the universe. In The Message of the Sphinx book, Graham Hancock, demonstrated that the dimension of the Great Pyramid and Earth are connected at a scale of 1:43,200. Likewise, the same is seen at the Stonehenge in England. Fulcanelli, the French alchemist and author of Le Mystère des Cathédrales, said that, "Saturn completes one Great Year of 25,920 years every 864 of its 'years', a half cycle every 432 of its 'years', a quarter cycle every 216 of its 'years', and an eighth of a cycle every 108 of its 'years'." As a result, 432 is significant in relation to 25,920 in the orbit of Saturn. 432 Hz also resonates with the Golden ratio and is a key number in sacred geometry. Its frequency was used by the Greek God of music, Mozart, Verdi, ancient Egyptians, and Tibetan monks. In addition, many famous composers used this hertz to create their master pieces. Finally, the 432 Hz is seen in the Golden ration found in nature and consistent with patterns of the universe.

The 528 Hertz resonates with the human body for repair and healing. It was used for blessings, miracles, and healing by ancient priests and civilizations. John Hutchinson, an electromagnetic energy expert from Vancouver, B.C., Canada, and his partner, Nancy Hutchinson (formerly Nancy Lazaryan) used the 528 Hz frequency and other Solfeggio tones to decrease the effects of the oil spill off the Gulf of Mexico in 2010. 528Hz is the bioenergy of health and harmonic vibration that re-connects our heart with the divine. On the contrary, low frequencies have a negative effect on the body, create blockages, and can dramatically shift our behaviour, create fatigue, headaches, lack of concentration, irritation, and possible harm to us. For example, many mobile operators use radiofrequency waves that are harmful to humans, and range in the 300 MHz to 3 GHz. One of the major reasons why there is so much anxiety, depression, autism, Alzheimer,

PTSD and so forth is partially because our brains are not in the right frequency patterns. Our brain is constantly trying to match its own wave pulse to sounds heard in our environments. As a result, this affects our brain and its performance and health. Repeatedly listening to 432 or 528 Hz will help train, heal, and calm the mind.

In conclusion, the Holistic methodology honours our soul connection. It nurtures and re-connects it through Holistic meditations and private consultations. We should deeply care and tune back to our soul to find joy, or can we get lost in our life maze and within ourselves, and lose or rupture our soul leaving us with a feeling of emptiness. In brief, we all have an essential light of life that we should re-connect with to shine.

CHAPTER 11:

Holistic Movement Exercises

The Holistic Movement exercises should be performed with awareness, breath, consciousness, emotion and feeling, and interconnection.

Every session starts by interconnecting the body, mind, and soul and adding breath to deepen the inner and the outer connections. Once this is established, a classical 15 minute warm up for the spine, the main path of our energy and life, is conducted. This is followed by warming up the right side then the left side of the upper body with breath, movement, and stretching. Subsequently, the hips and right and left legs are stretched and warmed up. Upon completion of the 15 minute warm up, the abdominals, legs and back are toned. At the end of every session one should end with the classical 3 arm circle exercise or with the Holistic meditation, to embrace one's body, mind, and connection to the inner-self and to the outer universe.

Warning: All exercises and information are provided in good faith for educational purposes only. Under no circumstances, the Holistic Movement employed concepts and exercises shall be held liable for any physical or mental harm. You should consult your physician or health care provider before starting any exercise program, especially if you have had any pre-existing injury, surgery, or physical condition that may cause, now or in the future, or might have caused in the past any type of previous physical or mental discomfort or health issue. The use of any Holistic movement exercises are solely to be performed at your own risk. Immediately stop all exercise and movements if you experience pain, nausea, dizziness, headache, heart and breathing discomfort, or feel unwell. Always honour your body, mind, soul, and own health.

Re-Connection

Purpose: The Re- Connection pose is used to enhance body, mind, soul connection to a higher field of energy and the universe. This pose helps reduce fear, stress, anxiety, worriedness, while manifesting our desires in a calm body and mind state. It can be performed anytime and anywhere for improved feelings of oneness, connection to oneself, and a higher source of power.

Instructions:

1. From standing position, interlace your fingers overhead, lengthen your spine, open chest, and gently tilt your head upwards to a slight upward angle.

2. Stay in the pose for 3-10 rounds of breath.

3. Re- affirm your desires such as health, love, and joy In the pose (For example: I am healthy, I attract love).

Heart Connection

Purpose: This pose is used to open heart, enhance emotions, heart feeling, and to re-connect to the Divine through the language of heart and love.

| **Position 1** | **Position 2** |

Instructions:

1. From standing position, place arms slightly behind hips, expand chest and heart, broaden shoulders, Position 1. Inhale deeply.

2. Exhale, expand spine, throat, chest upwards, lengthen arms upwards, reaching palms to sky, Position 2.

3. Repeat 3-10 repetitions with empowering positive affirmations from the heart (Example: I am love, I am kind, I am forgiving, I am grateful).

Spine Warm Up Exercises

In the Holistic Movement sequence, the spine is regarded as King and Queen of our body that must be unblocked in order to open up our energy, provide structure and support for body, and enable one to move freely with flexibility. The spine is vital for health, overall body flexibility, and nervous system function.

Half Body Roll

1. Begin in Re-Connection pose, inhale deeply.
2. Gently round spine forward half way with interlaced fingers, tucking belly inwards, exhale completely.
3. Perform 10 repetitions slowly with awareness to unblock the middle, upper spine from tension, stress, and fatigue.

Full Body Roll

Position 1   Position 2

1. Begin in Re-Connection pose, inhale deeply.
2. Gently round spine forward into Half Body Roll, slowly exhale.
3. Complete exhale and round spine to floor, open the lower, middle and upper back.
4. Perform 10 repetitions slowly with awareness to unblock the lower, middle, upper spine from tension, stress, and fatigue.

Star Connection

Purpose: This pose is perfect to download information, open 3rd eye point, crown chakra, calm mind, reduce stress.

1. From standing position, reach arms overhead, press palms firmly together, lengthen spine, throat, head upwards, while firmly grounding feet.

2. Inhale and exhale 3-5 rounds of full breaths.

3. Connect 3rd eye (between eyebrows) or forehead upwards receiving energy from external planets, stars, galaxies, or sun and moon.

Upper Body Warm Up

Right Arm Backwards Circle

Position 1

Position 2

Position 3

1. From Star Connection, Position 1, Inhale deeply.
2. Look forward, lengthen right arm forward, position 2, lengthen left arm upwards.
3. Circle right arm backwards, position 3, exhale.
4. Perform 10 repetitions.

Spinal Twist Right Side

Position 1

Position 2

Position 3

1. From standing position raise both arms upwards, position 1, draw shoulder blades downwards. Inhale.
2. Reach both arms forward, parallel to the ground, position 2, slightly exhale.
3. Fully twist spine right side as arms follow the spinal twist, position 3, complete exhale,
4. Return to position 1 and repeat position 2 to 3.
5. Perform 10 repetitions with breath.

Right Spinal Twist with left arm circle slap back

| Position 1 | Position 2 | Position 3 | Position 3 | Position 4 |

1. From Right Spinal Twist, position 1, expand your arms sideways, keep arms parallel to the floor, position 2. Inhale.

2. Circle left arm toward right arm in spinal twist position 3. Slightly exhale.

3. From position 3, lengthen both arms upwards in right spinal twist, position 4, completely exhale.

4. Return to position 1.

5. Repeat position 2,3,4 for 10 repetitions with breath.

6. Option: From position 4, circle both arms backwards, expand chest, perform 10 repetitions.

7. Return to star connection pose when done.

Star Connection

Left Arm Backwards Circle

| Position 1 | Position 2 | Position 3 |

1. From Star Connection, Position 1, Inhale deeply.
2. Lengthen right arm upward, reaching left arm forward parallel to floor.
3. Circle left arm backwards with exhale.
4. Perform 10 repetitions.

Spinal Twist Left Side

| Position 1 | Position 2 | Position 3 |

1. From standing position raise both arms upwards, position 1, drawing shoulder blades downwards. Inhale.
2. Reach both arms forward parallel to the ground, position 2, slightly exhale.
3. Fully twist spine to left side, as arms follow the spinal twist, position 3, completely exhale.
4. Return to position 1 and repeat position 2 to 3, 10 repetitions with breath.

Left Spinal Twist with right arm circle slap back

| Position 1 | Position 2 | Position 3 | Position 4 |

1. From Left Spinal Twist, position 1, expand your arms sideways parallel to the floor, position 2. Inhale.
2. Circle right arm toward left arm in spinal twist position 3. Slightly exhale.
3. From position 3, lengthen both arms upwards in left spinal twist, position 4, completely exhale.
4. Return to position 1.
5. Repeat position 2,3,4 as 1 sequences repetition. Repeat 10 repetitions with breath.
6. Option: From position 4, circle both arms backwards, expand chest, perform 10 repetitions.
7. Return to star connection pose when done.

Arm Scissors

| Position 1 | Position 2 |

1. From standing position, reach right arm upwards, position 1, and lower left arm downwards
2. Alternate arms to position 2.
3. Perform 20 repetitions alternating arms.

Center Chest Stretch

Position 1   Position 2

1. From standing position, reach both arms forward parallel to the floor, position 1. Inhale.

2. Expand both arms backwards shoulder height, stretching chest, position 2, exhale.

3. Repeat position 1 to 2 for 10 repetitions with breath.

Single Right Arm Chest Stretch

Position 1   Position 2

1. From standing position, reach both arms forward, position 1, parallel to floor. Inhale.

2. Stretch right arm backwards, lengthening left arm forwards, parallel to floor, position 2, exhale.

3. Perform 10 repetitions.

Single Left Arm Chest Stretch

Position 1

Position 2

1. From standing position, reach both arms forward, position 1, parallel to floor. Inhale.
2. Stretch left arm backwards, lengthening right arm forwards, parallel to floor, position 2. Exhale.
3. Repeat 10 repetitions.

Spinal Rotation Right Side

Position 1

Position 2

1. From standing position, bend arms in front of body, position 1, fingertips touch. Inhale.
2. Twist upper body and spine to the right side. Exhale.
3. Repeat 10 repetitions.
4. Option: On your 10th rep you can add pulse twists to open spine further, perform 10 repetitions.

Spinal Rotation Left Side

Position 1

Position 2

1. From standing position, bend arms in front of body, position 1, fingertips touch. Inhale.
2. Twist upper spine and body to the left side. Exhale.
3. Repeat 10 repetitions.
4. Option: On your 10th rep you can add pulse twists to open spine further, perform 10 repetitions.

Arm Circles

Position 1

Position 2

Position 3

1. From standing position, keep legs 1-3 feet apart, raise and lengthen both arms upwards, position 1. Inhale.
2. Circle both arms backwards, position 2, 3.
3. Perform 10 backward arm circles.
4. Perform 10 forward arm circles.

Left Side Stretch Series

Position 1

Position 2

A. Single left side stretch

1. From Star pose, position 1. Inhale.
2. Open legs 2-3 feet apart.
3. Lengthen left arm overheard stretching left torso, place right hand on knee, position 2. Exhale.
4. Perform position 1 to 2, 10 repetitions.

B. Left side stretch swing

1. From Star pose. Inhale.
2. Swing upper body to left side, reaching left arm overhead, relax right arm, engage core. Exhale.
3. Perform 10 repetitions.

C. Left side double arm stretch

1. From Star pose. Inhale.
2. Stretch both arms overhead to left side, engage and firm core. Exhale.
3. Perform 10 repetitions.

D. Split arm left side stretch

Position 1   Position 2

1. From Star pose. Inhale.
2. Lengthen left arm overhead to left side, while wrapping right arm behind back. Engage core. Exhale.
3. Perform 10 repetitions.

E. Left side ankle support stretch

Position 1   Position 2

1. From Split arm left side stretch, place right hand on ankle, position 1. Inhale and exhale naturally.
2. Pulse stretch the pose.
3. Perform 10 pulses.
4. Wrap left hand backwards, position 2, lengthen head to knee
5. Perform 10 repetitions.

Left Side Stretch Series

A. Single right side stretch

1. From Star pose, position 1. Inhale.

2. Lengthen right arm overheard stretching right torso, place left hand on knee, position 2, exhale and breathe naturally.

3. Return to star pose, position 1. Perform 10 repetitions.

Position 1   Position 2

B. Right side stretch swing

1. From Star pose. Inhale.

2. Stretch body to left side, reaching right arm overhead, relax left arm, engage core. Exhale.

3. Perform 10 repetitions.

C. Right side double arm stretch

1. From Star pose, inhale.
2. Stretch both arms overhead to right side, engage and firm core, exhale.
3. Perform 10 repetitions.

D. Split arm right side stretch

Position 1   Position 2

1. From Star pose, inhale.
2. Lengthen right arm overhead to right side, position 1.
3. Wrap right arm behind back, engage core and relax neck, position 2, exhale.
4. Perform 10 repetitions.

E. Right side ankle support stretch

1. From Split arm right side stretch, place left hand on ankle lengthen right hand upwards, position 1. Inhale and exhale naturally.

Position 1

2. Reach left hand overhead, position 2, perform 10 stretch pulses.

Position 2

3. Circle left hand backwards, position 3, lengthen neck and spine.

Position 3

4. Perform 10 repetitions.
5. Wrap right hand behind lower back, lengthen head to knee, position 4, hold stretch for 2-3 deep breaths.

Position 4

After completing the upper body side stretch series, the middle pelvis and lower body are warmed up and stretched. It is important to perform each exercise with awareness, consciousness, breath, and aim for your best range of motion to unblock the body.

Temple Pose

1. From standing position, lengthen spine and head upwards.

2. Keep arms to side of body, naturally stand tall, rolling shoulders back, and open chest.

3. Breathe naturally.

Temple Pose Long Neck Stretch

1. From Temple pose, raise elbows up and outwards with fingertips gently touching.

2. Lengthen neck and spine.

3. Breathe naturally.

Temple Pose Long Neck Stretch Hip Circles

1. From Temple pose long neck stretch, keep upper body still.
2. Circle hips right side, position 1, without moving arms and neck. Perform 10 repetitions.

Position 1

3. Circle hips left side, position 2, without moving arms and neck. Perform 10 repetitions.

Position 2

Temple Pose Long Neck Stretch – Single knee circles

| Position 1 | Position 2 | Position 3 | Position 4 | Position 5 |

1. Begin in Temple Pose Long Neck Stretch, position 1.
2. Raise right knee, position 2. Inhale.
3. Circle and open right knee outwards, position 3. Exhale.
4. Return to position 1. Perform 10 right knee circles, position 2,3, with breath.
5. Begin in Temple Pose Long Neck Stretch, position 1.
6. Raise left knee, position 4. Inhale.
7. Circle and open left knee outwards, position 5. Exhale.
8. Return to position 1. Perform 10 left knee circles, position 4,5, with breath.

Right Leg Stretch Series

A. Right Leg flat back stretch

1. From temple pose, pivot hips slightly to right side, place hands on knees, lock knees straight.
2. Lengthen spine parallel to ground, maintain a flat back.
3. Option: Pulse stretch 10 repetitions, or hold for 2-3 deep breaths.

B. Right Leg round back stretch

1. From right leg flat back stretch, grab right ankle, rounding back.
2. Lengthen spine and head downwards toward right foot.
3. Option: Pulse stretch 10 repetitions, or hold for 2-3 deep breaths.

C. Right Leg long back stretch

1. From right leg round back stretch, reach hands in front of right foot, lengthening spine forward.
2. Option: Pulse stretch 10 repetitions, or hold for 2-3 deep breaths.

D. Right Leg reach back stretch

1. From right leg long back stretch, tuck chin to chest, reach nose to knee.
2. Lengthen arms backwards towards back knee, keep arms parallel to ground.
3. Option: Pulse stretch 10 repetitions, or hold for 2-3 deep breaths.

Left Leg Stretch Series

A. Left Leg flat back stretch

1. From temple pose, pivot hips slightly to left side, place hands on knees, lock knees straight.
2. Lengthen spine parallel to ground, maintain a flat back.
3. Option: Pulse stretch 10 repetitions, or hold for 2-3 deep breaths.

B. Left Leg round back stretch

1. From left leg flat back stretch, grab left ankle.
2. Lengthen and round spine and head downwards toward left foot.
3. Option: Pulse stretch 10 repetitions, or hold for 2-3 deep breaths.

C. Left Leg long back stretch

1. From left leg round back stretch, lengthen arms forward around 1 foot in front of left foot.
2. Option: Pulse stretch 10 repetitions, or hold for 2-3 deep breaths.

D. Left Leg reach back stretch

1. From Left Leg Long Back Stretch, tuck chin to chest, reach nose to knee.
2. Lengthen arms to back knee, keep arms parallel to ground.
3. Option: Pulse stretch 10 repetitions, or hold for 2-3 deep breaths.

Center Legs Stretch Series

A. Flat Back

1. Open Legs widely several feet apart on the ground, place hands on knees.
2. Lengthen chest and spine forward into flat back.
3. Option: Pulse stretch 10 repetitions, or hold for 2-3 deep breaths.

B. Round Back

1. From Flat Back, relax head downwards and hold ankles with arms.
2. Release neck and spine tension, engage core.
3. Option: Pulse stretch 10 repetitions, or hold for 2-3 deep breaths.

C. Forward Long Spine Stretch

1. From Round Back, lengthen arms and torso to a slight forward diagonal stretch towards floor.

2. Place palms on floor.

3. Option: Pulse stretch 10 repetitions, or hold for 2-3 deep breaths.

D. Reverse Long Spine Stretch

1. From Forward Long Spine Stretch, reach arms backwards parallel to ground, position 1, engage core.

E. Forward Long Spine Stretch

1. Reach chest and arms to a slight forward diagonal towards floor, position 2.
2. Perform 10 repetitions from position 1 to 2 with natural breath.

F. Fly Forward Long Spine Stretch

1. From Forward Long Spine stretch, reach both arms simultaneously upwards, gently and naturally arching back.
2. Perform 10 repetitions from Long Spine stretch to Fly forward Long Spine Stretch.

Deep side lunge stretch series

A. Right knee deep lunge stretch series

Position 1

1. Bend right knee and sit into a deep low lunge with arms on floor, position 1.
2. Hold stretch for 2-3 deep breaths.
3. From position 1, reach arms upwards, lengthening spine and neck, position 2.

Position 2

4. Hold position 2 for 2-3 deep breaths.
5. From position 2, pivot upper body to right, place hands on floor, stretching back and hips, position 3.

Position 3

6. Hold position 3 for 2-3 deep breaths.

7. From position 3, place right hand near right foot on floor, and extend left hand overhead, position 4.

8. Hold position 4 for 2-3 deep breaths.

9. From position 4, place left hand parallel to right hand on floor, turn right knee forward, position 5.

Position 4

10. Hold position 5 for 2-3 deep breaths.

11. Wrap right arm behind lower back, expand chest, position 5.

Position 5

12. Hold position 5 for 2-3 deep breaths.

13. From position 5 pivot shoulders to right side, broaden chest, slightly arching spine, position 6.

Position 6

14. Hold position 6 for 2-3 deep breaths.

15. From position 6, lengthen right arm upwards, position 7, hold position for 2-3 deep breaths.

Position 7

B. Left knee deep lunge stretch series

Position 1

1. Bend left knee and lunge into a deep low lunge, position 1.
2. Place arms on floor, position 2.

Position 2

3. Hold stretch for 2-3 deep breaths.
4. From position 2, reach arms upwards, lengthening spine and neck to position 3.

Position 3

5. Hold position 3 for 2-3 deep breaths.
6. From position 3, place left hand on floor, position 4, extend right hand overhead.
7. Hold position 4 for 2-3 deep breaths.

Position 4

8. From position 4, pivot hips to left side into deep front lunge, position 5.

9. Extend spine and neck upwards.

10. Hold position 5 for 2-3 deep breaths.

Position 5

11. Wrap left arm behind lower back, broaden chest, place right arm near right foot, position 6.

Position 6

12. Hold position 6 for 2-3 deep breaths.

13. From position 6, gently twist spine to left, broaden chest, position 7.

Position 7

14. Hold position 7 for 2-3 deep breaths.

15. extend left hand upwards, position 8.

Position 8

16. Hold position 8 for 2-3 deep breaths.

Low Squat Series

Position 1

Position 2

1. From Temple pose, position 1, squat low, hands on the floor, position 2.

2. Broaden chest, shoulders, neck upwards, position 2, inhale.

3. Round and stretch spine in low squat, tucking chin to chest, position 3.

Position 3

4. Repeat 10 repetitions.

Body Roll Sequence

| Position 1 | Position 2 | Position 3 | Position 4 | Position 5 |

1. From Half Body Roll, position 1, engage core, exhale.
2. Slowly engage core, lengthening interlaced arms upwards, position 2, inhale.
3. Exhale, bow spine gently backwards, opening neck, chest, torso, position 3.
4. Inhale, side bend spine right side, position 4.
5. Exhale, side bend spine left side, position 5.
6. Return to temple pose.
7. Perform position 1 thru 5 for 5-10 repetitions.

Posture Opener

1. From standing position, interlace hands behind back. Round shoulders forward, engage core, position 1, exhale.

2. Expand chest, throat, spine upwards, position 2, inhale.

Position 1

Position 2

3. Repeat 10 repetitions with breath.

Holistic Core Training Exercises

Half Abdominal Rolls

1. Lie down on your back, arch back slightly, stretch arms overhead, bend knees with feet flat on the floor, position 1.

Position 1

2. Place hands behind head, expand ribcage, position 2, inhale.

Position 2

3. Lift head and shoulders toward thighs, engage core, rounding spine, position 3, exhale.

Position 3

4. Perform position 2 and 3 with breath, 10 repetitions.

Half Abdominal Rolls Left and Right Side

1. Begin in position 1, inhale.

Position 1

2. Pivot and round upper body to left side, engage core, exhale, position 2.

Position 2

3. Pivot upper body to center, position 1, inhale.
4. Pivot upper body to right side, engage core, rounding back, exhale.
5. Perform 10 repetitions for right side, and 10 repetitions for left side with breath.

Half Abdominal Rolls Long Legs

1. Lie down on your back, tuck knees into chest, place hands behind head, and lift head and shoulders toward knees, position 1, inhale.

Position 1

2. Exhale, touch elbows and knees, rounding upper back, position 2.

Position 2

3. Perform 10 repetitions from position 1 to 2.
4. From position 2, extend legs forward to a long diagonal, position 3.

Position 3

5. Perform 10 repetitions from position 2 to 3.
6. Rest

Half Abdominal Rolls Long Legs Right and Left Side

1. Lie down on your back, inhale, tuck knees into chest, hands behind head, reach right elbow to left knee, position 1, exhale.

Position 1

2. Inhale center.
3. Pivot upper body, and reach left elbow to right knee, position 2, exhale.
4. Perform position 1- 2, 10 repetitions.

Position 2

5. Return to position 1, exhale, lengthen legs forward to position 3, inhale.

Position 3

6. From position 3, inhale, pivot upper body to left side, exhale, position 4. Perform 10 repetitions for left and right side.
7. Rest

Flat Back

1. From seated position, raise arms equally up to sky, maintain straight spine, position 1, inhale.

Position 1

2. Tuck pelvis and core inwards, round back slowly to floor, position 2, exhale.

Position 2

3. Lie down on back, slightly stretch core and arch back, lengthen arms overhead, position 3, inhale.

Position 3

4. Perform 10 repetitions from position 1 to 3.

Single Right Arm Reach Flat Back, Knees Bent

1. From seated position, reach right arm upwards, straighten back, position 1, inhale.

Position 1

2. Roll spine half way, lengthen right arm forward, engage core, position 2, slightly exhale.

Position 2

3. Lie down on back, slightly arch spine, lengthen right arm overhead, position 3, inhale.

Position 3

4. Perform 10 repetitions from position 1 to 3.

Single Left Arm Reach Flat Back, Knees Bent

1. From seated position, reach left arm upwards, straighten back, position 1, inhale.

Position 1

2. Roll spine half way, lengthen left arm forward, engage core, position 2, slightly exhale.

Position 2

3. Lie down on back, slightly arch spine, lengthen left arm overhead, position 3, inhale.

Position 3

4. Perform 10 repetitions from position 1 thru 3.

Straight Back Right Arm Left Leg Reach

1. From seated position, extend left leg to a high diagonal, and reach right arm parallel to left leg.
2. Slowly engage core and roll back to floor and return back to seated position.
3. Perform 10 repetitions.

Straight Back Left Arm Right Leg Reach

1. From seated position, extend right leg to a high diagonal, and reach left arm parallel to right leg.
2. Slowly engage core and roll back to floor and return back to seated position.
3. Perform 10 repetitions.

Double Round Back

1. From seated position, bend knees to chest (feet off floor), lengthen arms overhead to straight back, position 1, inhale.

Position 1

2. Round back, elbows touch knees, position 2, reach arms forward parallel to floor, exhale slightly.

Position 2

3. Slowly roll down to position 3 and 4, complete exhale.

Position 3

Position 4

4. Perform 10 repetitions from position 1 thru 4.

Abs: Right Leg Reach Straight Back

1. Lie down on left side of body, reach legs forward to a 45 degree angle, engage core to position 1, inhale.

Position 1

2. Lift right leg to right arm, engage core, position 2, slightly exhale.

Position 2

3. Lift left leg to right leg, position 3, fully exhale.

Position 3

4. Slowly lower legs down and reach right arm back to stretch torso, chest, right arm, position 4, inhale.

Position 4

5. Perform 10 repetitions from position 1 thru 4.

Abs: Left Leg Reach Straight Back

1. Lie down on right side of body, reach legs forward to a 45 degree angle, engage core to position 1, inhale.

Position 1

2. Lift left leg to left arm, engage core, position 2, slightly exhale.

Position 2

3. Lift right leg to left leg, position 3, fully exhale.

Position 3

4. Slowly lower legs down and reach left arm back to stretch torso, chest, left arm, position 4, inhale.

Position 4

5. Perform 10 repetitions.

Lower Body Series

Hip Raises with high heels

1. Lie down on your back, bend and keep knees hip distance apart, reach arms to heals, position 1, inhale.

Position 1

2. Slowly engage and articulate core upwards, raise hips and heels, position 2, slightly exhale.

Position 2

3. Raise hips to maximum range of motion, fully exhale.

Position 3

4. Perform 10 repetitions from position 1 thru 3.

Frog Hip Raises with high heels

1. Lie down on your back, bend knees, reach arms to heals, position 1, inhale.

Position 1

2. Slowly engage and articulate core upwards, raise hips and heels, opening knees outwards, position 2, exhale.

Position 2

3. Perform 10 repetitions from position 1 thru 2.

Plie Side Bend

1. Squat low, open knees wide into a low plie stance, find balance on toes, broaden chest position 1, inhale.

Position 1

2. Exhale to standing, keep feet in plie position (heels together), engage core and side bend upper body to right side, position 2.

Position 2

3. Return to position 1.
4. Perform 10 repetitions from position 1-2.
5. Return to position 1.
6. Exhale to standing, keep feet in plie position (heels together), engage core and side bend upper body to left side, position 3.

Position 3

7. Return to position 1.
8. Rest

Mini Lunge Left Leg

1. From standing position, place left foot 2-3 feet in front of right foot.
2. Gently lunge low into a low mini lunge, round back, position 1, exhale.

Position 1

3. Gently articulate spine into straight back, lengthen arms forward parallel to floor, position 2, inhale.

Position 2

4. Raise spine and hips to starting standing position, and return to position 2.
5. Complete 10 repetitions.

Mini Lunge Right Leg

1. From standing position, place right foot 2-3 feet in front of left foot.

2. Gently lunge low into a mini lunge, round back, position 1, exhale.

Position 1

3. Gently articulate spine into straight back, lengthen arms forward parallel to floor, position 2, inhale.

Position 2

4. Raise spine and hips to starting standing position, and return to position 2.

5. Complete 10 repetitions.

Kneeling Left Leg Series

Left Leg Raises

1. From kneeling position place arms on floor, and raise left leg upwards to a high diagonal.
2. Engage core, broaden chest and shoulders.
3. Tap and lift left leg to floor and up to high diagonal.
4. Perform 10-20 repetitions with natural breath.

Left Bent Knee Raises

1. From Left Leg Raises, bend left leg to 90 degree angle.
2. Pulse left leg upwards.
3. Perform 10-20 repetitions with natural breath.

Left Knee Circles

Position 1   Position 2   Position 3

1. From Left Bent Knee Raises, engage core, circle left knee from position 1 to 2 to 3.
2. Perform 10 repetitions with natural breath.

Flying Left Leg Raise

1. From Left Leg Raise, lengthen arms forward, dipping chest downwards towards floor, balance.

Position 1

2. Hold stretch in position 1 for 3-5 deep breaths.
3. Bend left leg to 90 degree angle, position 2.

Position 2

4. Pulse left leg upwards, perform 10 repetitions.
5. Rest in resting pose, position 3.

Position 3

Kneeling Right Leg Series

Right Leg Raises

1. From kneeling position place arms on floor, and raise right leg upwards to a high diagonal.
2. Engage core, broaden chest and shoulders.
3. Tap and lift right leg to floor and up to high diagonal.
4. Perform 10 -20 repetitions with natural breath.

Right Bent Knee Raises

1. From Right Leg Raises, bend right leg to 90 degree angle.
2. Pulse right leg upwards.
3. Perform 10 repetitions with natural breath.

Right Knee Circles

Position 1   Position 2

1. From Right Bent Knee Raises, engage core, circle right knee from position 1 to 2
2. Perform 10 repetitions with natural breath.

Flying Right Leg Raise

1. From Right Leg Raise, lengthen arms forward, dipping chest downwards, balance.

Position 1

2. Hold stretch in position 1 for 3-5 deep breaths.
3. Bend right leg to 90 degree angle, position 2.

Position 2

4. Pulse right leg upwards, perform 10 repetitions.
5. Rest in resting pose, position 3.

Position 3

Holistic Upper Body Training

Flying Push Up

1. Lie down on your belly, legs together, and press palms on floor into position 1.

Position 1

2. Draw shoulders down, lengthen spine and neck, inhale.
3. Push upper body slightly off floor into position 2, slowly exhaling, engage core.

Position 2

4. Push body into push up position, bend elbows slightly, position 3, complete exhale.

Position 3

5. Perform 10 repetitions from position 1 thru 3.

Flying Triceps Push Up

1. Lie down on your belly, legs together, and press palms on floor into position 1, keep elbows near side ribcage.

Position 1

2. Draw shoulders down, lengthen spine and neck, inhale.

3. Push upper body slightly off floor into tricep push up position 2, slightly exhale, engage core.

Position 2

4. Push upper body up into position 3, engage core, fully exhale.

Position 3

5. Perform 10 repetitions from position 1 thru 3.

Holistic Back Series

Position 1   Position 2   Position 3   Position 4

Position 5   Position 6   Position 7   Position 8

Position 9   Position 10   Position 11

1. Lie down on your belly, keep legs together, lengthen arms forward.
2. Lift and lengthen right arm and neck upwards, engage back, position 1. Hold position 1 for 3-5 deep breaths.
3. From position 1, raise and lengthen left arm upwards, position 2.
4. Hold position 2 for 3-5 deep breaths.
5. From position 2, lengthen right arm on floor, raise left arm, position 3, for 2-3 deep breaths.
6. Reach both arms sideways, lengthening neck, lifting chest, position 4.
7. From position 4, reach fingertips near hips, lift and lengthen spine and chest upwards, position 5.
8. From position 5, lengthen both arms forward on the floor, drop chest, raise and lengthen right leg upwards, position 6, hold for 2-3 deep breaths.
9. From position 6, lower right leg, raise and lengthen left leg, position 7, hold for 2-3 deep breaths.
10. From position 7, raise right upwards, lower left leg reach toes backwards, lengthen arms forward, position 8.
11. From position 8, reach arms forward, raise both legs, position 9, hold for 2-3 deep breaths.
12. From position 9, reach arms backward parallel to floor, broaden chest, position 10, hold for 2-3 deep breaths.
13. Return to resting position 11 for 2-3 deep breaths.

Sprinter

Position 1

Position 2

1. From a low squat position, place arms on floor, lengthen spine, position 1, inhale.

2. Walk hands forward to full sprinter position on tip toes, engage core, lengthen spine, position 2, exhale.

3. Perform 10 repetitions from position 1-2 with breath.

Holistic Balancing Poses

Holistic balancing poses are important to conduct prior to stretching towards the end of a training session. Balancing poses are important to improve focus, concentration, prevent injury, prevent falls, improve overall body movement, reverse age related loss of balance, build posture, and improve muscular power and coordination.

In the Holistic methodology balancing exercises can be done statically or dynamically with repetition and breath.

Right Leg Balance Series

1. From standing position, or temple pose, raise and lengthen arms overhead.

2. Engage core, raise right leg to 90 degree angle, position 1, hold for 2-3 deep breaths.

3. Gently pivot right foot laterally to right side, position 2, hold for 2-3 deep breaths.

Position 1

Position 2

4. From position 2, balance, reach right foot back, open arms for balance, hold for 2-3 deep breaths.

Position 3

5. Perform 10 repetitions.

Left Leg Balance Series

1. From standing position, or temple pose, raise and lengthen arms overhead.

2. Engage core, raise left leg to 90 degree angle, position 1, hold for 2-3 deep breaths.

Position 1

3. Gently pivot left foot laterally to left side, position 2, hold for 2-3 deep breaths.

Position 2

4. From position 2, balance, reach left foot back, open arms for balance, hold for 2-3 deep breaths.

Position 3

5. Perform 10 repetitions.

Holistic Stretching

In the Holistic methodology, stretching is very important for progress and muscle maintenance. Stretching reduces injury, muscle tension, stress, improves posture, and promotes healthy, flexible, strong muscles with full range of motion in joints. All stretching movements generally begin with the spine, then lower body limbs, followed by upper body, and posture re-balancing exercises.

Round to Arch Back Series

1. Kneel into resting pose, with arms and head on floor, position 1. Take 2-3 deep breaths.

3. Inhale, arch back into position 3, broaden chest, shoulders, head upwards.

Position 1

Position 2

2. Slowly engage core, articulate spine and round spine into position 2, exhale.

4. Exhale, round upper back, keep arms straight under shoulders, position 4.

Position 3

Position 4

5. Return to position 1.
6. Perform 10 repetitions.

Seated Side Stretch

| Position 1 | Position 2 |

1. From seated position, gently sit slightly on heels, stretch left arm overhead twisting and lengthening spine, position 1, hold for 2-3 deep breaths.

2. From seated position, gently sit slightly heels, stretch right arm overhead twisting and lengthening spine, position 2, hold for 2-3 deep breaths.

3. Perform position 1 and 2 equally for total of 2-3 deep breaths for 1-3 repetitions.

Seated Right Leg Stretch Series

| Position 1 | Position 2 | Position 3 |

1. From seated position, lengthen spine upwards, bend and hold right leg close to chest keeping right foot on floor, position 1.

2. Gently pivot right leg into position 2, right knee facing forward. Keep spine upright.

3. Place left arm backwards on floor, lengthen right arm overhead, position 3, arching spine, lifting chest upwards, hold for 2-3 deep breaths.

4. Perform 5-8 repetitions.

Seated Left Leg Stretch Series

Position 1   Position 2   Position 3

1. From seated position, lengthen spine upwards, bend and hold left leg close to chest, keeping left foot on floor, position 1.

2. Gently pivot left leg into position 2, left knee faces forward.

3. Place right arm backwards on floor, lengthen left arm overhead, arching back, position 3, lifting chest upwards, hold for 2-3 deep breaths.

4. Perform 5-8 repetitions.

Holistic Posture

In the Holistic methodology, posture is viewed as important as emotion, body and mind training. Correct posture allows bones and joint to move in correct alignment so muscles may be properly used. Good posture also muscles to be used more efficiently, increases energy, digestion, blood circulation, makes you feel taller and more confident.

Holistic Posture Re-Connection

1. From standing position, interlace hands overhead, arching spine slightly (re-connection pose), position 1, inhale.

Position 1

2. Expand chest, neck and arms to a slight V shape diagonal, position 2, exhale.

Position 2

3. Perform 3-5 repetitions with natural breath.

Horse Stretch

1. Interlace hands behind back, broaden chest and shoulders, slightly step left leg forward and bend left knee, position 1.

3. Return to standing.

4. From standing position, interlace hands behind back, broaden chest and shoulders, bend right knee, position 3.

Position 1

Position 2

2. Slowly bow head forward to left knee, position 2, reach arms overhead. Hold for 2-3 deep breaths.

5. Slowly bow head forward to right knee, position 4, reaching arms overhead. Take 2-3 deep breaths.

Position 3

Position 4

6. Return to standing.
7. Perform 3-5 repetitions per leg (position 1-2 and position 3-4).

Holistic Ending

Every session or class is always completed with the 3 Arm Circle, to balance, re-connect, and re-align body, mind, and soul to oneself and with the universal field.

After completing the 3 Arm Circle, one can peacefully end their session in Holistic meditation.

Three Arm Circle

Position 1   Position 2   Position 3

1. Start from star pose position, standing straight, legs hip distance apart. Reach palms upwards pressing palms together overhead, position 1.

2. Think of 3 positive affirmations to close your session (Example: I attract health, I am love, I am powerful, I am happy, I am grateful etc…)

3. To empower your affirmations, close your eyes and visualize each affirmation with a visualization.

4. Slowly inhale, re-affirm and feel your visualization, circle and open your arms backwards, position 2, return hands slight behind hips, position 3.

5. Perform 3 repetitions with breath.

The Holistic movement exercises should generally be conducted in full sequence and order to remain in harmony with a balanced muscular structure, progress, tone, and build an upright posture. Removing or avoiding certain exercises for particular medical, health, or physical reasons is honoured, however; private sessions may be recommended for those students.

Modifications for all exercises can be done in all exercises if needed by bending various body limbs such as elbows, knees, or by decreasing the range of motion in stretching. With repetition and instruction, the body will naturally adapt to its original and an improved range of movement. Intermediate students can advance their practice by conducting the movements and exercise with speed, additional repetitions, and quicker transitions in between exercises. Upon completion, one is highly encouraged to engage in Chapter 15 meditation to re-balance and align body, mind, soul to oneself and the universe.

CHAPTER 12:

Rebuilding Emotions

In the Holistic methodology, emotional training and comprehension are as important as training the body and mind. Humans are emotional beings, and our emotions have evolved into 6-8 primary emotions that help us survive, communicate, and build relations. Our emotions are expressed through body language, verbal communication, facial expressions, or non-verbal means.

History of Emotions

The word emotion was adopted from the French word "émouvoir" and was presented into academic discussions in 1579. During that time, emotion was interpreted as passion, affections, appetites, sentiments. For example, people would have said and expressed I feel "first emotions of passion," which today could be understood as the emotion of happiness. The concept of emotion clearly did not exist. People felt other things such as passions, moral sentiments, accidents of the soul, and explained them very differently than how we understand emotions today. In 1800's, the word and concept of emotion emerged with Thomas Brown in the English language. During that century "emotion" meant body stirrings associated with mental feelings. For some medical and philosophical writers, the term "emotion" was reserved for those bodily stirrings that were viewed as the external signs of inward passions and affections.

Charles Darwin wrote <u>The Expression of the Emotions in Man and Animals</u> in 1872. Darwin supported his theory of evolution, by demonstrating the expressed emotions in his research. He believed that emotions consisted in reality of different emotions that were adapted and evolved at different times.

Darwin believed that humans and animals shared common behaviors. For example, if we look at our primal emotion of fear, it originated from our pre-mammal ancestors to survive. Fear is an ancient emotion that we still possess today. When we are in a fearful state, our eyes widen to increase our visual field and give our eyes the ability to move, find, and track threats. Other emotions, such as social nurturing and love, have been expressed for centuries between a mother and her child in animals and humans alike. In addition, social emotions, such as guilt and pride, evolved among social primates.

Expressed Emotions and Adaptive Functions

Expressed emotion	Initial physiological function	Evolved communicative function
Fear	Amplified visual field, bigger and quicker eye speed movement	Warning of potential threats. Appeasement to aggressor.
Surprise	Amplified visual field with widened eyes	More research required
Disgust	Tightening of facial muscles, decrease of unsafe inhalations	Warning of danger foods, actions, behaviors
Happiness	More research required	Absenteeism of danger
Sadness	More research required	Eye tears to show conciliation, gain compassion.
Anger	More research required	Warning of approaching threats, dominance.
Pride	Increased lung volume for meeting competitors	Enlarged social status
Shame	Decreases weak body areas from potential attacks	Reduced social status

In conclusion, the modern evolutionary theory - looking at the following table of emotions above, evolutionary psychologists consider human emotions have evolved and they were best adapted to our ancestors and our currents lives.

What Are Emotions?

Emotions are 'e-motions' in action that motivate us and increase our chances of survival. We are born with our adapted and evolved emotions.

Facial expressions are a universal system that expresses one's emotional state. According to <u>Oxford Dictionary</u> emotion is "A strong <u>feeling</u> deriving from one's circumstances, mood, or relationships with others."

Paul Ekman, an American psychologist and professor in the 20th century, identified seven basic emotions. He discovered that these seven universal facial expressions are equally expressed worldwide, regardless of culture and ethnicity. These facial expressions are: Fear, anger, sadness, joy, disgust, surprise, and trust. These expressions were defined as below:

Fear - feeling of being afraid, frightened, scared caused by danger, pain, threat, harm.
Anger - feeling angry, annoyance, or hostility.
Sadness - feeling sad, sorrow, unhappy.
Joy - feeling happy, great pleasure.
Disgust - feeling something is wrong or revolt, strong disapproval.
Surprise - being unprepared for something that could be astonishing.
Trust - a positive emotion expressing firm belief in the reliability of something or someone.

Facial Expression

Our emotions arise from the posterior superior temporal sulcus located on the right side of the brain. The amygdala, located in the lower part of the brain, has the ability to decipher emotions.

Facial expressions give one life, otherwise without them there would be no feeling. One's emotions can be affected by negative traumatic experiences such as violence, poverty, mental illness, substance abuse and more. Our control and emotion connection are as important as training the body and mind and can directly affect our well-being, health, energy, life, and decision making for an improved lifestyle.

Another prominent American professor and psychologist, in the early 19th century, was Robert Plutchik. He created the psycho evolutionary theory and contributed articles on emotions in the World Book Millennium 2000. Robert believed that humans have eight emotions versus Paul Ekman's belief that humans have seven primary emotions.

Plutchik believed humans have the following eight primary emotions: anger, fear, sadness, disgust, surprise, anticipation, trust, and joy. These emotions were believed to be triggered with a certain behaviour to survive. He developed his basic emotions psycho evolutionary theory with ten suggestions that include:

1. Emotion is applicable to animals and humans on all evolutionary levels.
2. Emotions have evolved into multiple forms of expression in different species.
3. Emotions are used to increase and handle survival issues for all living organisms.
4. Emotions and forms of expression that have common patterns and elements that can be identified in all living species.
5. There is a minor quantity of basic, primary, or prototype emotions.
6. All other emotions are mixed or copied states that occur as combinations of primary emotions.
7. Primary emotions are theoretical concepts that are inferred from different sorts of evidence.
8. Primary emotions can be theorized as pairs of polar opposites (example: joy-sadness, anger-fear, trust-distrust, surprise-anticipation).
9. Emotions vary in their degree or similarity to one another.
10. Emotions can exist in various degrees of intensity or levels.

Sample of Spiraling Wheel Of Emotions that give feeling, wisdom, power, vision

Plutchik's wheel of emotion is very helpful to clearly visualize and understand one's emotions and the emotion combination that create the final emotional outcome.

8 primary emotions are seen in the second circle and include anger, disgust, fear, sadness, anticipation, joy, surprise, and trust.

The wheel is characterized by colors, layers, and polar opposite emotion relation.

The eight primary emotions are arranged by colors that have high intensity. Emotions with a more faded color are a mix of the two primary emotions. The colors are used to demonstrate similar emotions.

In the layers section, the center of the circle and the color are intensified. For example, in the center of the wheel we can see primary emotions that change from anger to rage, anticipation to vigilance, joy to ecstasy, trust to admiration, fear to terror, surprise to amazement, sadness to grief, disgust to loathing. In the outer layers, the color and its

intensity fade to demonstrate that the emotion is decreased. In the outer layer we see love, submission, optimism, aggressiveness, contempt, remorse, disapproval, awe, and submission.

In terms of emotions and their relations, the spaces between the emotions demonstrate combinations when primary emotions mix. All polar emotions are opposite from each other. Their polar opposites can be seen as joy and sadness, fear and anger, surprise and anticipation, trust and disgust.

We can also see from the wheel that if we add anger and anticipation we get aggressiveness. If we add joy and anticipation, we get optimism. If we add joy and trust we get love. Trust and fear creates submission, fear and surprise create awe, and surprise and sadness create disappointment.

In conclusion, the wheel can be used as a 2 or 3 dimensional circle, and demonstrates the most common identifiable patterns and elements that make up each emotion.

"Emotion is defined as an episode of interrelated, synchronized changes in the state of all or most of the five organismic subsystems in response to the evaluation of an external or internal stimulus event as relevant to major concerns of the organism."

-Emotion Researcher, 2015

The Holistic emotional rebuilding classes and sessions focus on re-activating genuine feelings from the heart and enhance their expression through body language, facial expression, communication and so forth. These classes and sessions re-align and fine-tune emotions in order to re-balance and gain control over them. At the end of such classes or sessions, one feels a sense of emotional release and serenity, improved emotional connection and control and balance over one's emotions.

The Importance Of Emotions

Emotions affect our health, motivation, well being, senses of fulfilment and decision making.

Most people are stuck in a 9 or 10 year old state of consciousness because emotions begin to get suppressed by our environment, society, education, culture and more at that age. For example, a 15 year old teenager has a home curfew and must be home at 5 pm. Obviously the 15 year old would like to be out for longer, and does not emotionally accept this curfew. As a result, this may start to stir emotions for the 15 year old and create emotional conflict at home and emotions begin to get suppressed. Some 15 years may revolt, get angry or become aggressive and leave home because they do not agree with the 5 pm home curfew. The 15 year old teenagers may leave home for a few days, however; soon realizes that it is not easy to survive on their own, as there are larger world rules that they must followed as well. These rules can vary from the need for a job, a degree, or a supporting shelter if one does not want to end up homeless. As a result, the 15 year teenagers may decide that in their best interest if to return home. As they return home they are still holding onto many painful emotions due to the imposed curfew and try to escape. This could be manifested by substance abuse, aggressiveness, tantrums and so forth which could later evolve, due to their suppressed emotions, to other issues at an older age, such as workaholics, gym addiction, materialism, health issues.

In the Holistic emotional rebuilding classes and sessions emotions are re-balanced, expressed, and negative emotions are de-emphasized. The only two positive emotions that are emphasized in the holistic sessions are Joy and Trust which we will cover later in this chapter. Engaging in dance, music, art, exercise are always supported to help clear old and new emotional blockages. Awareness, control, and expression of our emotions help one gain inner peace and build an emotion repertoire that serve us in a positive way.

The Future of Emotions

Emotions give rise to human existence and should be honoured, trained, enhanced and controlled for a balanced and positive human life.

The future of our emotions will decrease as we de-attach from traditional human interactions, primitive socialization skills, and alter our verbalization and communication skills.

In addition, with increase in technology, our emotions will reach a stage where they may need to be re taught to regain emotional feeling in one's life. If we do not engage in positive human emotion, our world and humanity will be transformed with no feeling, health issues, increased negativity, unbalanced body, mind, soul, and be de-attached from the universal laws of human life.

It is important that we engage in emotions, feelings, and in the Holistic emotional re-building classes and sessions in order to regain our health, joy, and happiness in our life.

Holistic Emotional Exercises

To build a healthy balance emotional state one must practice emotional mastery with awareness, observation, training, learn wheel of emotions, and know the combination chart of mixed primary emotions. If these are practiced, the steps to rebuilding positive emotions become simple. The following Anderson's chart shows the primary emotion combinations.

Combination chart when primary emotions are mixed (Anderson, 2017).

Love	Joy + Trust	Remorse	Sadness + Disgust
Guilt	Joy + Fear	Envy	Sadness + Anger
Delight	Joy + Surprise	Pessimism	Sadness + Anticipation
Submission	Trust + Fear	Contempt	Disgust + Anger
Curiosity	Trust + Surprise	Cynicism	Disgust + Anticipation
Sentimentality	Trust + Sadness	Morbidness	Disgust + Joy
Awe	Fear + Surprise	Aggression	Anger + Anticipation
Despair	Fear + Sadness	Pride	Anger + Joy
Shame	Fear + Disgust	Dominance	Anger + Trust
Disappointment	Surprise + Sadness	Optimism	Anticipation + Joy
Unbelief	Surprise + Disgust	Hope	Anticipation + Trust
Outrage	Surprise + Anger	Anxiety	Anticipation + Fear

Exercise: Emotional Mastery for Anger

If we reflect on the wheel of emotions, we have learnt that annoyance leads to emotions of anger and rage. The opposite emotion of anger is fear. If we add anger and anticipation we get aggressiveness. Therefore, we must look at these emotions objectively. For example, if we are angry we must look at it objectively, and hold it tangibly in our mind as we engage in Holistic meditations, Holistic movement, or Holistic consultation sessions. Anger should be viewed as an entity that arises from an external stimuli and can be controlled once it is clearly visible as a tangible object. Once we can tangibly grasp the emotion of anger we can control and understand where it came from and replace or transform it.

To begin the exercise, follow the following steps.

1. State the stimuli. I am angry because………………….. (write what caused your anger).

2. Rate your anger. My anger is ……..(3 is the highest intense emotion of rage, 2 is emotion of aggressivity, and 1 is emotion of annoyance).

3. Practice Holistic meditation to calm and clear the mind for 5 minutes.

4. During your meditation practice, envision filling your mind with the opposite emotion of anger such as happiness. Focus on your new emotion of happiness and clearly visualize something that you are engaging in that makes you happy or joyful. As you continue your meditation you will feel the shift in our emotions. Your new positive mindset will be stronger and larger then anger. If you still do not feel that shift, add a couple extra minutes to your meditation.

5. Once you have entered a calm emotional state, rewind the video tape and see number 1, the stimuli, that caused your anger to be rated in number 2.

6. State to your subconscious, "I am in control of my emotions, and my positive emotions overtake my angry emotions. I am always positive. Good bye anger."

7. Visualize seeing the anger fade and travel away from you as you practice forgiveness, kindness, compassion, and love towards the stimuli.

8. Slowly open your eyes and be grateful for releasing negative emotions to improve your overall health and well being.

Emotional Re-Balance Test

1. Rate your 6 primary emotions (Number 3 is high intensity, 2 medium intensity, 1 not intense).

2. List the major stimuli,

3. Write the opposite positive emotion, and a positive affirmation with your opposite emotion that you can use during your meditation.

For example:

Emotion	Rate	Stimuli	Opposite Emotion	Affirmation
Disgust	3	Snakes	Admiration	I admire a snake's beauty

4. During your meditation, state: I admire snakes several times until the emotion of disgust decreases.

5. Re-affirm " I admire snake's beauty."

6. Visualize seeing the positive things of the snake such as its patterned designed, flexibility, strength and so forth.

   This should help change your perspective of snakes and decrease the rate of emotion. With private sessions and consultations this could be removed or completely altered.

7. Complete your chart:

Emotion	Rate	Stimuli	Opposite Emotion	Affirmation
Anger				
Disgust				
Fear				
Happiness				
Sadness				
Surprise				

8. Upon completion, use your new affirmations and repeat them 5-10 times during your Holistic meditation practice while visualizing and feeling your affirmation as in the previous example.

9. Practice until your emotion has faded or decreased in intensity.

Rebuilding Positive Emotions

In the Holistic methodology we focus on positive emotions. Our positive emotions are amplified and expressed in order to live harmoniously within the universal laws of life. As a result, this increases our health, overall well being, and internal balance and peace.

As you may recall, Plutchik stated that we have 8 primary emotions. Within the 8 emotions, the emotion of joy and trust are re-trained and emphasized for overall well being and positivity in the Holistic methodology.

"Joy and trust are the Holistic movements key emotions for a healthy and happy life."

-Julie Rammal

The other emotions are trained and re-balanced for individuals to gain emotions of joy and trust in their lives. This is provided in classes, consultations and sessions.

Exercise: Joy and Trust Emotional Mastery

1. To begin experiencing the emotion of joy and trust re-affirm to yourself daily the following:

   "I trust in the Divine, and trust that everything will happen in the right Divine order of time."

2. Upon completion of the re-affirmation, start to engage in the emotion of Joy. For example, look at the sky with joy, pick your favorite fruit from the supermarket with joy,, count your blessings and be grateful.

3. Re-affirm to yourself daily the following:

   "I am happy now, and attract joyful things."

4. Finally, try to smile more, ssurround yourself with positive things, and laugh more.

Exercise: Happy Facial Expression

1. Wake up every morning with a smile, and practice the happy facial expression daily re-affirming the following:

   "I am Joy, I am Happy."

2. To perform the happy facial expression, focus on one point in front of you, and slightly tilt chin downwards.

3. Gently squint eyes, and create an internal giggle or think of something funny.

4. Gently widen your mouth into a smile, showing your teeth.

In conclusion, joy and trust are amazing golden emotions that can lift our health, positivity, and well being. We should practice and engage our emotions with awareness, control, and understanding using the wheel power of emotions, combination chart of emotions, and joyful facial expressions in order to regain a positive and happy life, body and mind.

Chapter 13:

Attitude, Affirmations & Gratitude

Our power of attitude is important because it can take a negative or positive direction. The holistic methodology focuses on improving and training one's attitude to be: positive, persistent, loving, generous, merciful, optimistic, and to embrace life.

In the holistic methodology one is trained for every challenge in body, mind, soul and attitude to survive the life maze. This training can take months to years depending on one's: will power, determination, and discipline.

The entire birth of the holistic methodology, this book, and the DVD: In Light Of Change was built with a calling, and the right attitude to persist, be merciful, grateful, and to believe in the power of changing lives.

Likewise, Henry Ford went through many hardships before he built the Ford Motor Company. It was his attitude that made him successful. He persisted, had passion, curiosity, and believed in himself and his work.

"If you think you can do a thing, or can't do a thing, you're right."

-Henry Ford

Attitude is either negative or positive, but can never be neutral. It is an expression of positive or negative evaluation of our environment, people, things, or events. In the holistic methodology students are taught to induce a positive attitude which translates to success in themselves and their lives. If your attitude is positive and optimistic you will succeed, however; if it is negative success is less tangible. In the holistic methodology one is taught to believe and have the attitude of, "It can be done." Students who train with: fear, lack of faith, giving up, confusion, and negative attitudes will not make it in the holistic methodology. The entire is system is designed to challenge all levels of the body, mind, soul, emotions, and attitude to create, awaken, and empower individuals. This is why the holistic methodology was first accepted and used by the 1% percent population because it was originally a luxury sport that was used to transform the body, mind, subconscious and one's life and attitude. It has the power to reset the entire human system, remove ego, and improve: power, success, relation, visibility and so forth. The power of this movement is much more powerful than just training the body, mind and soul, it is the power that gives you life.

What Are Attitudes?

Our attitudes are a learned tendency to evaluate events, people, things and so forth. According to the ABC model of attitude, we have the following three elements: affective, behavioural, and cognitive.

Our attitudes are created when we observe or experience something, and can be altered by reprograming our attitude response. For example, we may gain emotion of a topic (affective), which drives us to behave a certain way (behavioral), and later forms a belief of what we experienced (cognitive).

Attitude is mental energy that reflects our thoughts, feelings, emotions, actions, and directed our behaviour. It is based on past behaviour, our attitudes on that behaviour, and it is function on subjective norms (what others think), our intentions, and lastly our willingness to engage in our behaviour.

In the Holistic methodology attitude is a product of beliefs, and it is everything. A student can only improve, grow and transform with the right attitude that is aligned with the universe. A student's attitude is trained and practiced to: believe in oneself, be positive, optimistic, open, curious, kind, caring, and loving and supportive when needed. Such attitudes help one cope with the laws of life, enriches optimism, remove negative thoughts, and can make one feel happier and successful.

A Lion and Tiger's Attitude

If we look at animals and study the behaviour of a lion and tiger, the lion is the the king of the animal kingdom, and yet the tiger is stronger than the lion. The lion is respected, and has a strong leader attitude. Other animals in the jungle may fear the lion because of its attitude, and leadership behaviour. The lion acts like it thinks, and is king because of what it believes in himself. In the holistic methodology students are taught to believe in themselves, and their behaviors are modified to have the right attitude in every circumstance that is presented.

If we look at the tiger, this special animal lives mostly alone in solitary, and is stronger that the lion. This research has been recently expressed in the conservation charity 'Save China's Tigers.' As a spirit animal, the tiger is willpower, personal strength, and courage. The Chinese God Of Wealth, Tsai Shen Yeh, emphasizes his power by usually sitting on top a tiger. The tiger has always been perceived as power, yet aggressive when needed to be.

As a result, the Holistic methodology respects and honors both animals character, and believes that one should be a lion and a tiger when needed.

Get The Right Holistic Attitude

In the Holistic methodology, one is trained to avoid negative events and people, explore their passion, think positively, control emotions, set goals, never give up, remove excuses, be grateful, believe, have faith, gain knowledge, and re-connect with the universal laws of human life. However; when necessary the tiger attitude must exist by defending oneself, acting, protecting only in defence and when needed. We must allow yang to dominate our characters, but know that the yin is also there, otherwise with only yang we can not co-exist in this upcoming century.

"Your attitude, not your aptitude, will determine your altitude."
-Zig Ziglar

Through the holistic methodology and movement, one is trained to practice positive and negative attitude exercises, and is trained how to balance and use both under various circumstances.

The attitude of every student is everything in the holistic classroom.

Food For Attitude

Food is very important because if our attitude with food is not correct, we will suffer.

Our food should be our source for positive memories and experiences. One is taught to eat for positivity, to connect to their food, and observe how it is consumed. Eating should be a positive practice, that should engage our sense of taste, smell, and sight rather than a product of emotional comfort or release. Several wonderful superfoods to enrich our well being are Chia seeds, acai, maca, goji berries, raw nuts, and green tea. There benefits include:

Chia Seeds: Cleansing, detoxification for body

Acai: Improves brain function, eliminates harmful toxins

Maca – Stress reducer, energy and hormone balancer

Goji berries – Improve immune system, focus, and vision

Raw nuts- High in protein, nutrients, antioxidants and good fats

Green Tea – Fat loss, Brain focus, overall health benefits

Our attitudes with food are very important because if the elements of control and quantity, gratitude, generosity, awareness, and observation are not practiced with food, the student is lacking the right attitude with food. In the holistic methodology, food is perceived as a need to survive, that is appreciated, natural, nutritious and proportionate to our physical, mental needs rather than our emotional needs.

In conclusion, the holistic methodology and our attitude of ourselves, life, food, people, environments must be trained to be: optimistic and positive, or one would be failing themselves, and their lives. Attitude is one of the key's to success, be open, curious, persist, and you will win.

Holistic Affirmations for Transformation

Affirmations are a powerful way to create new beliefs with repetition, and remove negative self sabotaging thoughts. They can be used anywhere, anytime, however; it is always best to say it with feeling from the heart in our quiet meditative spaces.

Affirmations help reprogram the brain, the subconscious mind, and alter our old beliefs to create the world we truly desire. Affirmations are also energy that is sent to the universe, and can be chanted audibly or silently spoken depending on one's feelings. A few great positive affirmations for all of humanity that can be used daily are:

I am an amazing.

I am a human being who spreads love.

I have a beautiful sparkling soul.

I am divine love.

I am happy.

I attract positivity everywhere I go.

I am positive.

I love life, and spread joy everywhere.

I am grateful for everything.

My heart is always filled with love and peace.

I am joy.

I am open to all universal blessings.

My life is blessed.

I trust in the universe.

I always have faith and hope.

My body, mind and soul are in harmony.

I am in control of my body, mind and spirit.

I am blessed.

I can always find a way.

I am beautiful.

I spread light wherever I go.

I am always thankful for everything.

Everything is great.

Life is amazing and beautiful.

I am valued and appreciated.

I spread gratitude and kindness.

The Power of Gratitude

Gratitude is a positive emotion that comes from appreciation, and is important because it makes us kinder, more appreciated, and people honor this behaviour.

Gratitude is essential to having and living our lives. It is so powerful, because it is the highest resonating frequency that is equal to joy and love. In the holistic methodology students are taught to express gratitude by clapping their hands, saying thank you, or showing appreciation. When such behaviour is practiced, we are only speaking the universal language which invites us to receive more joy, happiness, and abundance.

How to Be Grateful

Gratitude can be expressed by saying by using words, celebrating, gathering, writing or more. The most used words to express gratitude are thank you, thank you so much, I appreciate it, I truly recognize your efforts, I am grateful.

Traditional past rooted approaches to express gratitude were seen by indigenous people that did and still do: service, prayer, conduct parades or festivals and celebrate holidays such as the Thanksgiving holiday.

For example, in Ghana the Ewe people have a Yam Festival with food, music and dances to celebrate the first appearance of yams at the end of the rainy season. In 1621, the Plymouth colonists and Wampanoag celebrated Thanksgiving to give thanks to the creator for the harvest and blessings. Similarly, the harvest Fruit Fair in Thailand is celebrate in gratitude for their beautiful exotic fruits that are presented in extravagant arrangements.

The easiest way to be grateful is to always say thank you whether something is good or bad, as the practice of gratitude lifts your vibration and connects you higher with the universal laws of life.

Everyday, we should be grateful for having this moment, day, opportunity to breathe, eat, bathe and so forth. We should always count our blessings, and practice gratitude for happiness, joy, and abundance.

The Gratitude Test

To improve your gratitude skills, practice saying thank you every morning to the universe for all that you see and have. With practice and time, add and share more gratitude words, behaviour and action to people, things, animals, and your environment by saying, "Thank you, I appreciate you, I am grateful." For example, when you wake up in the morning, say "Thank you for the sun and light." Everything around us loves respect, appreciate, and being appreciated.

"The power of gratitude has the power to change the world and everything within it."

-Julie

When we practice gratitude as part of our living, our world would be more peaceful and loving.

CHAPTER 14:

Love & Universal Meditation

Love is the most powerful force in the world, and the holistic methodology is the love of the human race and the body, mind and soul. Without love, there is no joy, genuine happiness, and everything in our body, mind and spirit get distorted or separated.

"Self love, and the love to everything around us, brings us: joy, health, and abundance."
-Julie Rammal

Each human has an amazing power of love within themselves that is connected to the Divine's love. Love is an unexplainable inner force that can empower the human race, through the use of its magical healing powers and uplifting vibrations. Love is an inner energy that must be re-nourished and cared for properly. It gravitates people together to transform and grow.

Humans have to be aware of this internal and powerful energy that can powerfully bound humanity together, empower them, and enlighten them to enter the highest field of energy if practiced.

How To Be Love

To be love, we must understand, accept and access this powerful inner energy through loving behaviours, thoughts, actions, and self-love. Throughout history, humans and numerous texts wrote and spoke of the power of love. For example, love was expressed in historical monuments such as the Taj Mahal which is one of the world's seven wonders. Mughal Emperor Shah Jahan built Taj Mahal to express his love to his late wife. In brief, the human race should express and practice true love to uplift their heart powers, vibrations, and entire connection to the universe. Love is the only language that the Divine understands.

Despite our frequent dis-connection to love, the love energy is always inside us, despite it is sometimes partially or entirely sub-pressed. Love could remain: open, semi-open, or closed. Humans must open and re-connect to their love power by being love, expressing love, and loving themselves first. When we love ourselves in body, mind, soul, and we love to attract and share, we experience joy, serenity, creativity, and happiness,. Love is the best feeling one could ever embrace, and should be re-opened, practiced, and stay the primary dominant part of ourselves.

Each one of us is light, has love, and is connected to the Divine's love. In fact, we are love and light before we are physical human beings with a body and mind. This incredible power is seen in almost every new-born. A new-born is so simple in form, peaceful, loving, bonding, and beautiful in perfection when awake or asleep. Children are innocent, pure love, shining light, and full of positivity, forgiveness, and kindness. Their behaviours change, as they grow up, affected by their environments, people surrounded with, and so forth, as they start living from their conscious minds.

We can practice "to be love", by creating and nurturing a healthy positive mind, body and soul through the holistic methodology, holistic home spa rituals, holistic meditation and by acting like love. We should practice the expression of love in everything we do from work, connecting with people, relationships, and engaging in our talents. Love gives us an immense power to excel in our life maze, when it originates purely from our inner source of genuine love. For example, we should eat our food with love and feeling, or care for our family, children, plants, animals, nature, Earth, people and so forth. Our actions could multiply our inner love force, and expand outward to everything we touch, encounter, or absorb in our lives. It is like a magic wand that enlightens every heart with an incredible force.

Unfortunately, love is decreasing and changing its form through technology, social media, emoji's, and love proposals, such as on Instagram and other applications. Despite all, love will always find its way because it is a positive vibration. Love can only and truly be expressed, felt, and absorbed in the traditional approaches that the body, mind and soul are accustomed to. For example, love can be expressed with a human hug, but this feeling can not be equally expressed with an emoji hug in virtual ecosystems. These artificial ecosystems can pose immense risks that can drown us in loneliness, suppression of our true emotions or dis-orienting them to be fake. This is increasingly hurting and suppressing the human heart as we become dis-connected on how to use our heart and love.

The change in our approach, on how we express and communicate love, is separating and isolating body from our soul. In Japan, for example, this change has sparked the government's fear that people will not marry anymore due to the extremely sophisticated online and virtual world communication systems. Another example, Dubai created the Ministry of Happiness to re-teach people the feeling of happiness. What is happening in Japan, Dubai and in other countries could be soon spread out further to become a worldwide love epidemic. Our emotions may soon have to be boosted with applications or gadgets to feel what is love, happiness, joy and so forth.

"Your life begins when your heart is open."
-Julie Rammal

In conclusion, love should always be expressed in traditional holistic approaches, by sharing a real emotion such as a hug, or a smile from the heart. Our lack of connection to real emotions of love could deprive, de-balance, and de-attach our entire body, mind and soul and disconnect us from the laws of life and the divine. If one re-awakens their heart and inner love, and expresses it outwards naturally, magnificent miracles and happiness, health, youthfulness, and joy will be enhanced.

Universal and Love Meditation

The Universal and Love meditation have been prepared for individuals to uplift their vibrations and spread the positive light of change.

One could use the Universal and Love Meditation to re-connect, embrace the positive changes, improve vibration, bless negativity, spread positivity, health, joy, creativity, and energy to oneself and to the world.

Universal Meditation Exercise

From a comfortable seated position, use the holistic breath to find your peace and connection to yourself and the divine. Once you feel your body, mind, and soul are inter-connected and you have entered a higher state of consciousness, read the below passage a few times before closing your eyes in meditation.

I am light,

I am love,

I am compassion,

I am kindness,

I am forgiving,

I am grateful,

I am the child of the universe.

My light spreads:

Love, compassion, kindness, forgiveness, and gratitude.

I am the light of change.

My light expands indefinitely with the Divine.

When done reading the passage, close your eyes, and envision seeing your energy, and aura expanding with light of: positivity, love, compassion, gratitude, kindness, forgiveness, and re-connecting upwards to the divine. Embrace this connection with one minute of natural holistic breathing. Feel your new vibration, power, and thank the universe for all of your blessings, growth, wisdom, life, and love. Once done, open your eyes, and smile to the universe's beauties.

"Kindness is a language that the deaf can hear and the blind can see."
- Mark Twain

Universal Love Meditation Exercise

From a comfortable seated or a standing position, soften your gaze and read the following lines out loud or silently in your heart:

I am love,

I am in love,

I am in love with the universe and with all of its possessions and inhabitants.

My love spreads and sparks the love in each person.

My love is my gift to be used to empower the human race,
myself, family, and re-connect to the Divine's Love.

I act with love, and I am the light of love.

When done, slowly re-connect back to your external world, and place a positive oldies love song and dance and express the love that you will spread. You will feel an immense joy, happiness, childlike connection, and may even laugh while dancing. Life is supposed to be fun, joyous and loving.

In conclusion, love keeps one's vibration high. Love is our source to health, happiness, joy, abundance and connection to everything within and around us. Although during our lifetime, we may witness some traumatic and evil things, we should forgive, and uplift our love powers by practicing the holistic methodology to spread: love, compassion, kindness, forgiveness, gratitude and be the love and light of change.

Good luck in your practice, learnings, and teachings.

"Be the light of change, and your light will spread out."
-Julie Rammal

Printed in the United States
by Baker & Taylor Publisher Services